Learning
Disability Today

Key issues for providers, managers, practitioners and users

Edited by Steven Carnaby

Learning Disability Today
Key issues for providers, managers, practitioners and users

Edited by Steven Carnaby

© Pavilion Publishing (Brighton) Ltd, 2007

Published by
Pavilion Publishing (Brighton) Ltd
Richmond House
Richmond Road
Brighton
East Sussex BN2 3RL
Tel: 01273 623222
Fax: 01273 625526
Email: info@pavpub.com
Web: www.pavpub.com

First published 2007.

A catalogue record for this book is available from the British Library.

ISBN: 978 1 84196 224 5

Pavilion is the leading training and development provider and publisher in the health, social care and allied fields, providing a range of innovative training solutions underpinned by sound research and professional values. We aim to put our customers first, through excellent customer service and good value.

Pavilion editor: Bonnie Craig
Cover and page design: Anthony Pitt, Pavilion
Cover image: Susan Moyle
Printed on paper from a sustainable resource by Hartington Litho Limited

Contents

Part three   Shaping lives together

Foreword

I am pleased to write the foreword to this revised and updated edition of *Learning Disability Today*. This handbook will provide a new generation with inspiration and information as they tackle the urgent tasks of consolidating new ways of working with people with learning disabilities. The white paper, Valuing People, set the direction but it is publications such as this that enable the vision to be translated into 'on the ground' services for people and fed through into appropriate and equitable support for them, and for their families.

This handbook provides a thorough introduction to recent developments in the policy and legal framework, changes that have acted as drivers for partnership working and anti-oppressive practice. It sets out a balanced and evidence-based approach to a range of important areas of practice, including behaviour that challenges, seeking good mental and physical health care and the more contentious issues such as sexuality, safety from abuse, choice making, risk and parenthood. The particular needs of people with autistic spectrum disorders and/or profound and multiple impairments, and of older people with learning disabilities, are addressed so that those in need of a high level of support are not inadvertently excluded from recent developments (Brown, 2004) or marginalised within the learning disability community. Skills such as good communication, record keeping, advocacy and sensitive planning are described because these underpin good relationships just as much as the expert knowledge, which is here in abundance.

In the field of learning disabilities it is easy to keep reinventing the wheel, each time setting off hopefully with a new set of terminology and then falling into disillusionment when the same old difficulties re-emerge. That is why it is so important that this handbook brings together such a broad range of expertise and commitment, providing those working in the field with the skills as well as the vision to address the real issues with integrity.

Reference

Brown H (2004) *Community Living for People with Disabilities in Need of a High Level of Support*. Strasbourg: Council of Europe.

About the contributors

Peter Baker is a Consultant Clinical Psychologist working for Sussex Partnership NHS Trust and is responsible for the intensive support service for people with learning disabilities who present challenging behaviour. He is also an Honorary Senior Lecturer at the Tizard Centre, University of Kent. In both of these roles he is a passionate exponent of positive behavioural support, advocating person-centred approaches and 'getting lives' for the people he serves. He has published widely on the subjects of challenging behaviour and social inclusion of people with learning disabilities.

Jill Bradshaw trained as a Speech and Language Therapist, working with adults with learning disabilities and challenging behaviour. As her research interests increased she went to work at the Tizard Centre as a Lecturer in learning disabilities, where she contributed to the centre's teaching, research and consultancy work. She has published work on staff communication, communication and challenging behaviour, active support and training staff to work with people with challenging behaviour. She is currently completing her PhD in staff views of communication and challenging behaviour at Manchester Metropolitan University and has an honorary post as Lecturer at the Tizard Centre, University of Kent.

Alison Brammer is Senior Lecturer in Law at Keele University. Previously, she worked as a Solicitor in local government, specialising in social services matters, including childcare, mental health and registered homes tribunals. She is Director of the MA in Childcare Law and Practice at Keele University and teaches social work law. She has written numerous articles considering the law relating to vulnerable adults in various settings and has written legal articles in *Learning Disability Review* (published in association with the Tizard Centre). She currently writes a legal column for *The Journal of Adult Protection*. Her book, *Social Work Law*, is published by Pearson. Alison has been involved in extensive training of social services and health sector personnel.

Hilary Brown is Professor of Social Care at Salomons, a faculty of Canterbury Christ Church University, having previously held a Chair at the School of Health and Social Welfare at the Open University and a senior post at the Tizard Centre, University of Kent. She has worked on issues of sexuality and abuse in learning disability services for many years through research, teaching and policy development, including work about men with learning disabilities who are at risk of sexually offending and the needs of people with learning disabilities who are dying. In recent years she has focused on the abuse of all vulnerable adults, consulting to local authorities, national bodies such as the National Patient Safety Agency and the Public Guardianship Office, as well as to international bodies including the Council of Europe. She is also training to be a psychotherapist and is interested in the mental health of people with learning disabilities and their access to mainstream support services.

Paul Cambridge is a Senior Lecturer in Learning Disability at the Tizard Centre, University of Kent. He has also worked as a Researcher in local government and at the Personal Social Services Research Unit. He has undertaken research on the long-term outcomes and costs of community care, deinstitutionalisation, sexuality and adult protection. His publications cover the sexuality and sexual health of men with learning disabilities, intimate and personal care, deinstitutionalisation, commissioning, care management and adult protection. He recently completed an evaluation of the specialist adult protection co-ordinator role and, with other colleagues at the Tizard Centre, is looking at the adult protection referrals and related data on process and outcomes held by Kent and Medway social services departments.

Steven Carnaby is Consultant Clinical Psychologist with Westminster Learning Disability Partnership and Honorary Lecturer in Learning Disability at the Tizard Centre, University of Kent. He has worked with people with learning disabilities for over 20 years and published work about their lives in areas such as service design and person-centred planning. Clinical interests include services for people with behaviour that challenges, support for people with autism and the development of systemic approaches to working with service users and their supporters. He is joint Editor of *Learning Disability Review* journal and editor of The British Psychological Society's Faculty for Learning Disabilities publication *Clinical Psychology and People with Learning Disabilities*.

Andrew Carpenter works for Penderels Trust as the Direct Payments Officer, funded by the Westminster Learning Disability Partnership. He has been in post since December 2004 and works closely with the Partnership to assist in the setting up and management of direct payments packages. Andrew's work has also included looking at ways to ensure that as many people with a learning disability as possible are able to access the direct payments scheme. This has included the use of user-controlled trusts and supported bank accounts.

Angela Cole is a freelance Consultant with more than 20 years' experience working in services for people with learning difficulties. She has worked in a range of settings and roles – from direct support to social work, and lecturing on service management and commissioning. Since going freelance, Angela has undertaken review and development work around the country and has been very involved in supporting the implementation of person-centred planning in a number of services. Angela is active in her local community alongside people with learning difficulties as well as in her work.

Mo Eyeoyibo is a Specialist Registrar in the Psychiatry of Learning Disability based at York Clinic, Guy's Hospital. He has experience in working with people with learning disabilities who have mental health problems and has worked both in the community setting and in specialist learning disability inpatient services. His areas of interest include research in the forensic aspects of learning disability and he is currently working on projects in this area. He enjoys teaching and contributes to the local postgraduate programme. Mo is a Governor of Nash College, school for people with physical and learning disability in the Borough of Bromley.

Gemma Gray is a Principal Clinical Psychologist with Ridgeway Partnership (Oxfordshire Learning Disability NHS Trust). Her areas of clinical interest and expertise are parents with learning disabilities, capacity and consent (including the Mental Capacity Act, 2005) and people with profound and multiple learning disabilities. She has extensive clinical experience working with parents with learning disabilities and their families and frequently acts as an expert witness with these families when they are in care proceedings. She also teaches widely on the subject. She is Secretary to The British Psychological Society Faculty for Learning Disabilities.

Geraldine Holt is Honorary Senior Lecturer in Psychiatry at the Institute of Psychiatry, King's College Hospital London, and Consultant Psychiatrist in Learning Disabilities at South London and Maudsley NHS Trust. She has published widely on the mental health of people with learning disabilities and serves on a number of national and international bodies with this focus.

Frank Keating is Senior Lecturer in Social Work at Royal Holloway, University of London. He completed a major review of mental health services for African and Caribbean communities published by the Sainsbury Centre for Mental Health (Breaking Circles of Fear: A review of the relationship between mental health services and African and Caribbean communities). As a result of this work, Frank serves on one of the national boards that oversee the implementation of the Department of Health's National Programme for Delivering Race Equality in Mental Health Services.

Claudia Linton used to work with children with a learning disability and profound and complex needs. From this, Claudia expanded her work to older people and adults with a learning disability. Claudia works in Westminster Learning Disability Partnership and has worked in a day service, developing skills in using alternative communication, promoting self-advocacy and advocacy. Claudia's current role is Person-centred Planning Information Officer. Claudia has developed training and facilitation for support staff who are leading person-centred planning in Westminster. In addition, Claudia has enhanced skills in making information more accessible with and for people with a learning disability.

Ann Lloyd is Integrated Commissioning Manager with the London Borough of Newham. She has worked in community-based services, promoting inclusion for people with learning difficulties. As a Job Trainer with A Chance to Work, she supported men and women with severe learning difficulties and complex needs into real jobs. She has worked as a Staff Development Officer helping staff gain the skills needed to support the moving-on process during the closure of a hospital for people with learning difficulties. In 1995 she led a team in setting up Hackney Community Resource Service, a community-based team supporting people to realise ordinary goals.

Henrik Lynggaard is a Chartered Clinical Psychologist with Camden and Islington Mental Health NHS Trust in London. Originally from Denmark, he has trained and worked mainly in the UK, where he has developed a strong interest in adapting systemic and narrative approaches in his conversations with people with learning disabilities. He is Co-editor of *Intellectual Disabilities: A systemic approach* published by Karnac books.

Marian Marsham is the Practice Development Nurse with Westminster Learning Disability Partnership, leading the Learning Disability Nursing team. She is also a student at King's College London on the MSc Advanced Practice (Leadership) course. She has had a broad professional experience with adults and children with learning disabilities across a range of settings and roles. She has a passion for promoting healthcare practice excellence, and cites her professional interest as making things better for people by getting the best out of them.

Michelle McCarthy is a Senior Lecturer in Learning Disability at the Tizard Centre, University of Kent. She has worked in the sexuality and learning disability field for many years and has a particular interest in working with women. She has written widely about her work in the professional and academic press.

Annette McDonald has over 20 years' experience in direct service provision for a wide range of client groups in differing settings and roles. She has been very involved in the development of self-advocacy for people with learning disabilities, and was instrumental in the setting up of a successful independent advocacy organisation, monitoring the quality of residential service provision. She published the training resource Home Alone (Pavilion, 2001) aimed at home care providers who support older people with dementia to continue to live in the community.

Peter McGill has worked in learning disability for 30 years, initially as an Instructor, Residential Social Worker and Clinical Psychologist. During this period he helped to establish community-based opportunities for people coming out of institutions. He joined the Tizard Centre, University of Kent in 1986 and was Director from 1999–2004. His interests now centre on challenging behaviour. He developed a Diploma course at the University of Kent, which has trained over 200 practitioners from all over the UK in systematic ways of working with people labelled as challenging. He is an author of over 50 articles, chapters and books on learning disability.

Hazel Morgan led the Foundation for People with Learning Disabilities from its creation in 1998. Her work with the Foundation includes key areas such as choice, mental health, working with families and spirituality. Previously, she was a lecturer in further and higher education. Her younger son, Peter, had severe learning disabilities. In his lifetime she wrote a number of articles from the perspective of a family carer and a book, *Through Peter's Eyes* (Hyperion Books, 1990).

Zenobia Nadirshaw is a Senior Qualified Practitioner with over 30 years of experience in the National Health Service. She has well-rounded clinical research and managerial experience relating to and influencing service planning, service provision and service delivery issues at local and national levels. A Clinical Psychologist by profession, she has impacted at national and European levels on issues of discrimination, equality and social inclusion within the professional education of psychology and nursing – including core competencies, knowledge and skills in training, selection and recruitment of multi-professional groups. She has won awards from The British Psychological Society and the British Medical Association.

Sally Powis works as a Clinical Psychologist with adults with a learning disability in South Oxfordshire for the Ridgeway Trust (formerly Oxfordshire

Learning Disability NHS Trust). She has a particular enthusiasm and interest in autistic spectrum disorders, having worked with both children and adults over the past 10 years, from those with severe learning disabilities and autism to those with Asperger's syndrome. Her experience of working with people with autism has included assessment and diagnosis, individual therapy, advising service providers, involvement in local autism service planning, training for staff and other professionals and research.

Lisa Poynor has 25 years' experience as a Registered Learning Disability Nurse, 14 of which have been supporting people with learning disabilities (and their families and carers) in her role as Community Nurse. She holds a BSc (Hons) in Specialist Practice (Community Learning Disability Nursing) and currently works for Surrey and Borders Partnership NHS Trust. She has previously published in the area of health promotion for women with learning disability, and has developed health promotion materials relating to a variety of topics. Her professional interests focus on facilitating access to primary healthcare, and health promotion.

Catherine Slater was born in London of an Indian father and an American mother. She lived in India from age seven until she returned to London when she was 12. She has an MA in history from the University of Cambridge, where she met her husband. She has three grown-up children. Her younger daughter, Karen, has Down's syndrome. Since Karen's birth Cathy has been active in various disability organisations and has a strong belief in inclusion and disability rights. Having been told when Karen was born that she would live in a residential home and work in a sheltered workshop, she eventually realised that Karen could have the opportunity to prove the experts wrong and live a full and independent life. Like her sister, brother and parents, Karen went to college, and like her sister then went on to leave the parental nest.

Karen Slater was born on 13 May 1979. She has a sister, Eli and a brother. She went to a mainstream playgroup and attended a special school part time. When she was five she started full time at the special school, Queen Elizabeth II Jubilee School. When she was 18 she went away to Derwen College, where she studied art, practical skills, candle-making, and other skills and enjoyed the social life, particularly the juke box and discos. In 2004 she moved into her own flat where she has support staff funded by direct payments. During the day she goes to a variety of adult education classes, which have included art, music, relaxation and massage among others. In the evenings she attends various youth clubs and on Sundays is a member of a soccer team called STEPS. She is an excellent photographer, enjoys bowling, music – especially Eminem – and travel.

Jennie Williams has a background in social psychology and a professional training in clinical psychology; she has worked as a Clinician for Health Authorities in Devon and Kent. Inequality and women's mental health has been a major theme in her work since the 1970s. In 1982 she was awarded a PhD for her thesis 'Gender and the Mental Health of Women', and she has continued to publish in this field since then. Jennie has many years' experience of helping mental health staff – through teaching, training and consultancy – to take inequality seriously and to work through the implications for their work with women with mental health needs. As a result of her concern about the safety of mental health services, she helped establish the Prevention of Professional Abuse Network (POPAN), a national organisation that aims to protect the interests of clients receiving therapy and other care services.

Introduction

When *Learning Disability Today* was first published in 2002, the key message from the white paper relating to people with learning disabilities, Valuing People, underpinned the material throughout the handbook:

> *'Improving the lives of people with learning disabilities requires commitment, nationally and locally, to strong principles, a firm value base and clear objectives for services.'* (Department of Health, 2001)

How far have we come with this commitment'? In 2005 Stephen Ladyman, Parliamentary Under Secretary of State for Community, stated that:

> *'The careful preparation and thought that went into developing the white paper and its implementation strategy is paying off. Experience so far suggests that this strategy, with its emphasis on independence, choice, inclusion and civil rights is standing the test of time. The framework it offers should go on delivering improvements for people with learning disabilities and their family carers for many more years. Valuing People has been groundbreaking in its insistence on putting people with learning disabilities and their family carers at the centre of the picture.'*

Putting people at the *'centre of the picture'* remains the most important objective for everybody supporting people with learning disabilities. The contributors to this revised and updated second edition of *Learning Disability Today* have endeavoured to achieve this in a number of ways – for example, by thinking about support from the service user's perspective, including examples of good practice in their discussions, or in some cases co-writing their chapters with authors who have learning disabilities.

The first edition of *Learning Disability Today* also emphasised the importance of partnership between people with learning disabilities, their families and carers, and the services available to support them. This commitment is now more important than ever as an increasing number of people with significant and complex needs are living – quite rightly – in the community as valued citizens, supported by increasingly creative and person-centred models. Valuing People's cornerstones of rights, independence, choice and inclusion for every individual now need to be interpreted carefully and meaningfully in order to support everybody safely and in personally relevant ways.

As in the first edition, this handbook has been divided into three main sections. The first, **setting the scene**, provides historical background as well as a discussion of the values, ideology and legislation underpinning current learning disability provision. Being more aware of our own position in society and what we personally bring to the service setting is essential to good practice, and such awareness is likely to enhance the collaboration between supporters and those being supported. This understanding of context is linked to an understanding of our role and accompanying responsibilities within vital areas, such as adult protection. Similarly, acknowledgement of the issues relating to the vulnerability of people with learning disabilities within risk management helps to ensure that we support autonomy and individual expression, and avoid the development of oppressive practices.

The second section of the handbook looks at ways of **developing people**. These chapters include pointers for good practice, enabling readers to apply some of the important ideas and principles set out in the first section. A new chapter on autism has been included, along with a very practical chapter with a range of ideas for supporting people with learning disabilities to keep physically healthy.

The final section looks at the ways in which together, people with learning disabilities and their supporters are **shaping lives**. These chapters discuss some of the challenges and aspirations faced by everybody, and how people with learning disabilities can be supported to make their own choices and ultimately have the freedom and support to live their lives. Throughout this section the emphasis is on developing inclusive practices that are built on the values and principles established in earlier chapters of the handbook.

The first edition of *Learning Disability Today* cited a key statement from Valuing People: *'Each individual should have the support and opportunity to be the person he or she wants to be.'* While progress has certainly been made since 2002, there is still a long way to go before we can say that this vision has been realised. It is hoped that this revised edition of *Learning Disability Today* will help readers continue to develop and expand their important role in making this happen.

Reference

Department of Health (2001) *Valuing People: A new strategy for learning disability for the 21st century.* London: Department of Health.

Acknowledgements

The production of this book relied on the efforts and support of a wide range of people. My thanks go to all of the contributors for their hard work and commitment to producing high quality material, and to Bonnie Craig and Jo Sharrocks at Pavilion Publishing for their advice, guidance and patience at various points during the production process. I am also grateful to Jonathan Bromberger for his invaluable support and encouragement while I have been working on this project.

The terms 'learning disabilities' and 'learning difficulties' are used interchangeably in this handbook. The editor acknowledges the debate on terminology and accepts the authors' preference on the use of terms.

Part one
Setting the scene

Chapter 1

The bigger picture
Understanding approaches to learning disability

Key words
acquired, consensus, impairment, lucidity, psychometric assessment, containment, significant social functioning, block treatment

People with learning disabilities form one of the most vulnerable groups in society. Individuals vary significantly in the degree and nature of their disabilities. This variation in the kind of disability people have, and how extreme it is, means that we need to support people to lead their daily lives in a variety of ways, designed to meet their specific needs.

As an introduction to the important issues raised in the handbook, this chapter first summarises current thinking about the term 'learning disabilities', looking at its definition and how scientific knowledge continues to establish its causes. Second, there is discussion of how people with learning disabilities have been perceived through history, culminating in current thinking about 'good support'.

What is 'learning disability'?
According to the Department of Health (1998), a diagnosis of learning disability is given when an individual meets three important criteria, in that they have:
- a significant impairment of **intelligence**, as well as
- a significant impairment of **social functioning**, and that
- both of these impairments were **acquired** *before* **adulthood**.

Level of intelligence

A person's 'level of intelligence' is determined by a psychometric assessment (usually administered by a clinical psychologist). This provides a numerical measure of intelligence (an IQ score). A 'significant impairment' is indicated by an IQ score of below 70 (the average for the general population is 100).

Social functioning

'Social functioning' means the individual's ability to cope on a day-to-day basis with the demands of their environment. This includes skills in communication, self-care, home living, social relationships, using community resources (eg. shops and cafes), work, leisure, health and safety.

Having a '**significant impairment**' in social functioning suggests that the individual needs significant help to ensure survival and/or with social and community adaptation.

Acquired before adulthood

'Acquired before adulthood' means that the impairment was acquired before the age of 18 years. In practice, most learning disabilities are present at birth or have an onset in early childhood.

What causes learning disability?

The causes of learning disability are divided into three categories.

1 Those occurring before the child is born (**prenatal causes**).
2 Those occurring during birth itself (**perinatal causes**).
3 Those occurring after birth (**postnatal causes**).

The causes and descriptions listed in *Table 1* prevent the brain from developing in the normal way, which in turn causes problems with thinking and learning. There may also be other problems eg. physical disability, sensory impairments, epilepsy and so on.

Values and attitudes towards people with learning disabilities

The way that society sees people with learning disabilities has changed over time. It is important to think about the values that underpin these changes, as these same values also inform the services that support people with learning disabilities and influence how workers provide support.

Table 1: Causes of learning disability

Cause	Syndromes	Examples
Prenatal causes	Genetic syndromes	Down's syndrome; fragile X syndrome
	Other syndromes	Spina bifida; cerebral palsy
	Environmental factors	Malnutrition; drugs; alcohol; diseases
Perinatal causes	Biomedical factors	Infections in the womb (such as toxoplasmosis)
	Environmental factors	Asphyxia; premature birth; other difficulties during labour/delivery
Postnatal causes	Biomedical factors	Epilepsy; meningitis; Rett's syndrome
	Environmental factors	Head injury; lead/mercury poisoning; malnutrition; social deprivation

Figure 1 (overleaf) shows a way of understanding how these influences work:

- **People** supporting the individual 'interpret' and assess what that individual needs in the way of care.
- The ways in which this process happens is likely to be influenced by the values of the **organisation** that employs the staff member.
- In turn, the organisation designs services in ways that reflect the wider values prevalent in **society.**

These '**layers of influence**' are dynamic in that each layer influences, and is influenced by, those around it. The values inherent within each of the layers are fluid – there is not a 'right' way of providing support to vulnerable people. Good support is agreed on and arrived at by consensus. Increasingly, services use the evidence from research studies to inform how they work, and to establish principles of good support that underpin their practices. This scientific approach is relatively new – the following review of how people with learning disabilities have been supported in the past shows how values and attitudes have changed and the importance of understanding the power of **societal values** in providing health and social care.

Figure 1: Supporting an individual with learning disabilities – layers of influence

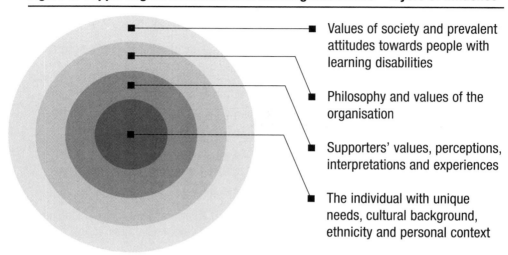

Values of society and prevalent attitudes towards people with learning disabilities

Philosophy and values of the organisation

Supporters' values, perceptions, interpretations and experiences

The individual with unique needs, cultural background, ethnicity and personal context

A brief history of service provision for people with learning disabilities

Language: idiots and lunatics

Changes in approaches to people with learning disabilities can be charted by tracing changes in the language used to describe them. From medieval times through to the late 19th century, the legal system distinguished between 'lunacy' and 'idiocy'. The term 'lunacy' referred to individuals with mental health problems (ie. people with problematic behaviour that was acquired, with periods of 'lucidity'). 'Idiocy' was used to describe individuals with learning disabilities, recognised as an irreversible state originating at birth. 'Idiots' were supported by family members receiving poor law relief, or by 'keepers' who provided lodgings and care.

Asylums and workhouses: safety, education and understanding?

The Victorian era saw a significant change. Asylums were created with the aim of educating people with learning disabilities and realising their potential. However, the number of people identified as needing this kind of service was greatly underestimated, and the asylums soon became overcrowded. The solution was to house people with learning disabilities in workhouses and alongside people with mental health problems. Medical professionals began taking over, and emphasis was placed on diagnosis and classification, rather than on social care and education.

The advent of industrial society saw further change and increasing hostility towards people with learning disabilities. Work became the centre of daily life, and the drive towards maximising production made no provision for slower individuals who needed more support to achieve the same outcomes as their peers. Everyday living was harsh, and those who could not keep up were despised. Those in power became concerned about people with learning disabilities having children of their own, advocating sterilisation and the repression of sexuality – a reflection of the values observed in wider society at that time. Institutional care therefore served as a means of containing people who were seen as worthless and unable to contribute to society, and segregated this group from the rest of 'productive' society.

From institution to community

The first half of the 20th century saw some changes in legislation, but little changed in the way of provision. In many ways, people with learning disabilities – or 'the mentally handicapped' – were largely forgotten. However, the post-war period saw the development of the NHS and other landmark reforms, such as the Children Act (1948), which argued that all children should be given the opportunity of experiencing a normal life. For many, this is the root of the move towards 'ordinary' living for those individuals previously subjected to a segregated, institutionalised lifestyle.

The 1971 white paper, Better Services for the Mentally Handicapped, established the idea of moving people with learning disabilities back into the community. This approach gained pace with the discovery of several scandals in the institutions, which revealed the extent of the poor living conditions and harsh, block treatment that people with learning disabilities had endured, largely unnoticed. However, it was not until the 1980s and the Community Care Act (1990) that a clear pathway for making provision in the community was outlined, and the major task of closing the mental handicap hospitals began in earnest. The development of community services has relied on a number of key ideas, described below.

Key ideas: normalisation, age-appropriateness and developmental models

Normalisation
Understanding normalisation

The majority of services supporting people with learning disabilities in Britain are heavily influenced by 'normalisation'. Care plans, operational policies, training in good practice – everything to do with quality provision has normalisation at its foundation. But what is 'normalisation'?

Defining normalisation: the Scandinavian roots

The majority of the literature concerning normalisation acknowledges that the roots of the approach lie with the Danish Mental Retardation Act (1959), which aimed to *'create an existence for the mentally retarded as close to normal living conditions as possible'* (Bank-Mikkelsen, 1980).

According to Bank-Mikkelsen (1980), the objective of 'making normal' was extended to housing, education, work and leisure, all built on an underlying theme of campaigning for the equality of human and legal rights for all citizens. Throughout the 1960s, such thinking led to major developments in learning disability services in Denmark and Sweden. The aim became to:

> *'(make) available to all mentally retarded people patterns of life and conditions of everyday living which are as close as possible to the regular circumstances and ways of life of society'* (Nirje, 1980).

In practice, this required that people with learning disabilities be enabled to experience the 'norms' of everyday life. For example, experiencing the rhythm of the day (we go to bed at night and get up in the mornings) and the week (most people work during the week and rest at the weekend).

Normalisation also demanded the acknowledgement that people with learning disabilities pass through the lifecycle, like others in the general population, and have the right to form relationships and experience an acceptable standard of living.

Developing the idea of normalisation: Wolfensberger's definition

The social and political environment in the USA was receptive to the ideas of normalisation, leading to widespread acceptance of the approach. Developments in civil rights activism, along with the acceptance by the federal courts of the 'least restrictive alternative' approach to psychiatric care helped a sociologist named Wolf Wolfensberger to formulate his ideas. His central definition of normalisation is:

> *'the utilisation of means which are as culturally normative as possible, in order to establish and/or maintain personal behaviors and characteristics which are as culturally normative as possible'* (Wolfensberger, 1972).

Wolfensberger initiated two important changes to the approach.

1 He refers to the way in which **society** views and represents people with disabilities.
2 He emphasises 'socially valued roles' – this led to the later renaming of normalisation by Wolfensberger as **social role valorisation (SRV)**.

Wolfensberger's normalisation therefore became a way of encouraging services to create a positive image for and with people with learning disabilities, aimed at decreasing their stigmatisation and increasing their acceptance by wider society.

Normalisation in Britain

The climate became right for the acceptance of normalisation in Britain in a similar way to events leading up to its establishment in North America. In addition, a series of scandals provoking investigations into living conditions in a number of long-stay institutions enabled normalisation to influence the design of new service provision, as well as the modification of existing institutions.

During the 1970s and 1980s organisations, such as the Campaign for Mentally Handicapped People and the King's Fund, built on evidence from research to provide strong support for an approach that advocated 'ordinary' lives for people with learning disabilities. Interpretations of normalisation in Britain tend to use John O'Brien's **five service accomplishments** to inform services.

1 **Community presence:** ensuring that service users are present in the same parts of the community as people without disabilities, be it at work or in recreational activity.
2 **Choice:** supporting people in making choices about their lives in as many areas, and including as many issues, as possible.
3 **Competence:** encouraging the development of skills and abilities that are meaningful to the immediate culture, skills that decrease a person's dependency and are valued by non-disabled people.
4 **Respect:** increasing the respect given to service users by other members of the community by ensuring that the lifestyles of people

with learning disabilities encourage a positive image to be conveyed to others. This might refer to the clothes that people wear, the places they go to, and the way that support staff talk to service users.

5 Participation: supporting people with learning disabilities in sustaining relationships with members of their family, as well as forming new relationships with others, ie. ensuring that '*service users participate in the life of the community*' (O'Brien & Tyne, 1981).

O'Brien's work can be said to be different from that of Wolfensberger only in that he leaves out references to sociological theory, and concentrates on **quality of life** and **lifestyle**.

Age-appropriateness

Services for people with learning disabilities throughout Britain share a common goal: to support the integration of people with learning disabilities into the local community. Linked with this is the idea of age-appropriateness – treating adults with learning disabilities *as adults*. Historically, people with learning disabilities were denied certain rights as adults, such as the right to make choices, the right to live a sexual life and the right to respect. Age-appropriateness is a way of ensuring that the support offered to people is appropriate to the individual's age.

Examples of age-appropriate support

- When the individual achieves something, saying '*Well done [person's name]!*' (rather than saying '*Good boy/girl!*').
- Setting up systems within a residential service whereby people are supported to buy their own food and pay their own rent (rather than food arriving in bulk and bills being paid by staff without any involvement of service users).
- People wearing clothes worn by people of their age in the general population (rather than an individual in their fifties wearing jogging bottoms and trainers all the time because it is easier for staff to support the person getting dressed).

The pros and cons

Age-appropriateness has been valuable in helping those supporting people with learning disabilities to gain a more positive image in society and access opportunities that are available to people without disabilities. The closure of institutions has made people with learning disabilities more visible, making it even more important for the general public to be educated.

However, it is also important that people with learning *disabilities* are respected for their *abilities*. There is a risk that by emphasising age-appropriateness above everything else, individuals with learning disabilities can be excluded from participating in activities and other aspects of community life because – for them – it is not meaningful.

The developmental approach

A way of tackling the thorny issue of age-appropriateness is to always have respect for the individual at the forefront of your mind. Respect for the individual means respecting *their* understanding of the world and the skills they have acquired for interacting with the environment. People with severe and profound learning disabilities, because of the level of their disabilities, are at the very early stages of development. While they are adults, and have lived a lifetime of experiences as an adult, the ways in which they understand the world and interact with it are at a level that can be compared to somebody much younger. Being aware of an individual's level of social and intellectual development is part of a person-centred approach to supporting them: starting with *who* the person is and *how* they can best be supported.

Summary

From birth, learning disability affects the way that people think and learn, and results in them needing varying levels of support to participate in daily life. The ways in which people with learning disabilities have been supported has changed dramatically throughout history. A major change has been the shift from segregated containment and block treatment to the more recent individualised approach that aims to place the person with learning disabilities and his/her needs and skills at the centre of any support that is provided.

The challenge for those working in services for people with learning disabilities is to provide support that strikes a balance between treating the individual appropriately as an adult, and ensuring that s/he can access the environment in meaningful ways. The best way to do this will be explored in later chapters in this handbook.

Further reading

Atkinson D, McCarthy M, Walmsley J, Cooper M, Rolph S, Barette P, Coventry M and Ferris G (Eds) (2000) *Good Times, Bad Times: Women with learning difficulties telling their stories.* Kidderminster: BILD.

Brown H and Smith H (Eds) (1992) *Normalisation: A reader for the nineties.* London: Routledge.

Forrester-Jones R, Carpenter J, Cambridge P, Tate P, Hallam A, Knapp M and Beecham J (2002) The quality of life of people 12 years after resettlement from long-stay hospitals: users' views on their living environment, daily activities and future aspirations. *Disability and Society* **17** (7) 741–758.

Forrester-Jones R, Cambridge P, Carpenter J, Tate A, Beecham J, Hallam A, Knapp M, Coolen-Schrijner P and Wooff D (2006) The social networks of people with learning disabilities living in the community 12 years after resettling from long-stay hospital. *Journal of Applied Research in Intellectual Disability* **19** (4) 285–295.

Myers F, Ager A, Kerr P and Myles S (1998) Outside looking in? Studies of the community integration of people with learning disabilities. *Disability and Society* **133** (3) 389–343.

Oliver M (1990) *The Politics of Disablement*. London: Macmillan.

BILD: www.bild.org.uk

The Foundation for People with Learning Disabilities: www.learningdisabilities.org.uk

Mencap: www.mencap.org.uk

References

Bank-Mikkelsen N (1980) Denmark. In: RJ Flynn and KE Nitsch (Eds) *Normalisation, Social Integration and Community Services*. Austin, Texas: Pro-Ed.

Department of Health (1998) *Signposts for Success in Commissioning and Providing Health Services for People with Learning Disabilities*. London: HMSO.

Ladyman S (2005) Foreword. In: Valuing People Support Team (2005) *The Story So Far… Valuing people: a new strategy for learning disability for the 21st century*. London: Department of Health.

Nirje B (1980) The normalisation principle. In: RJ Flynn and KE Nitsch (Eds) *Normalisation, Social Integration and Community Services*. Austin, Texas: Pro-Ed.

O'Brien J and Tyne A (1981) *The Principle of Normalisation: A foundation for effective services*. London: Campaign for Mentally Handicapped People: Community and Mental Handicap Educational and Research Association.

Wolfensberger W (1972) *Normalization: The principle of normalization in human services*. Toronto: National Institute on Mental Retardation.

Chapter 2

In context

Policy and legislation

Key words
collaborative working, policy initiatives, quality protects, rights-based approach, capacity

In order to be effective in working collaboratively with people with learning disabilities and their families, we need to be fully aware of the legal and policy context within which we are working. This chapter sets out the key legislative and policy initiatives that are likely to have direct impact on the lives of people with learning disabilities and summarises their main characteristics. It also contains a brief account of different service models for both children and adults with learning disabilities.

Developing a 'rights'-based approach
The law has tended to take a rather paternalistic stance towards people with learning disabilities, focusing on service provision. However, recent developments in the form of the Disability Discrimination Acts (1995 and 2005), the Human Rights Act (1998) and the Mental Capacity Act (2005) may promote and encourage development of a rights-based approach within law and practice affecting people with learning disabilities.

Legislation and service provision for children with learning disabilities

Legislation

The Children Act (1989)

The Children Act (1989) was a major piece of reforming legislation. The central feature of the Act is the welfare principle, which states that the child's welfare is the court's 'paramount' (most important) consideration. It also places great emphasis on the provision of local authority support for children and their families, to enable children to remain living with their families and avoid the need for formal proceedings. Support is targeted at 'children in need', which includes children with disabilities. Local authorities are required to *'provide services designed... to minimise the effect on disabled children... of their disabilities, and to give such children the opportunity to lead lives as normal as possible'*. These responsibilities are enhanced by the Quality Protects Initiative (1998), which includes a range of objectives and performance indicators for local authorities.

> ## Quality Protects Initiative
> Particularly relevant to children with disabilities is objective six, which aims to ensure that *'Children with specific social needs arising out of a disability are living in families or other appropriate settings in the community where their assessed needs are adequately met and reviewed.'*

The performance of local authorities with social services functions is now measured against 'performance assessment framework indicators'. Indicator CF/E67 measures:

> *'The number of disabled children supported in their families or living independently, receiving services in the census week, as a percentage of the estimated total population of disabled children in the council area.'*

The rationale for this indicator is that disabled children and their families should expect to be provided with services to meet their needs, and that if only a small proportion of families use social care services, it might suggest that services are difficult to access or unavailable (CSCI, 2005).

The Children Act (2004)

New legislation in the form of the Children Act (2004) was introduced following the Laming Report (Laming, 2003) into the death of Victoria Climbié. It provides statutory underpinning to the five outcomes for children identified as part of the Every Child Matters: Change for children programme, namely: be healthy; stay safe; enjoy and achieve; make a positive contribution; achieve economic well-being. The outcomes are intended to apply to all children, including children with disabilities, to improve well-being. The Act provides structural changes for the delivery of services to children and families. Children's services authorities have been established including education, as well as social services, functions for safeguarding children boards. There are new duties of co-operation on local authorities and other agencies to improve children's well-being and make arrangements to safeguard and promote welfare. Local safeguarding children boards have been established in place of area child protection committees. The Act also creates a new post of children's commissioner with the role of promoting the views and interests of children.

Within central government, responsibility for children's services and policies has moved to the Department for Education and Skills.

The Education Act (1993) (part 3) and (1996) (part 4)

Education law is complex and rapidly changing.

> ### The Education Act (1993)
> A key provision is the requirement that local authorities and schools identify, assess, record, meet and review special educational needs.

Other agencies must contribute to this process. A revised special educational needs (SEN) Code of Practice and SEN Toolkit supports the SEN provisions of the Special Educational Needs and Disability Act (2001). The Act and Code emphasise the importance of both working in partnership with parents and pupil participation. In future, a statement will normally only be issued when provision cannot reasonably be provided within normal resources. It is presumed that a child with special educational needs should normally have their needs met in a mainstream setting. At January 2005 around 1.2 million pupils were recorded as having special needs but no statement, and 242,600 had statements of SEN. If the education authority decides not to make a statement for a child, the child's parent may challenge this by appealing to the Special Educational Needs and Disability Tribunal. Every school should have a SEN co-ordinator (SENCO) and each child with SEN will have an individual education plan.

Legislation in Northern Ireland is similar to that in England and Wales. The Education Act (Northern Ireland Order, 1996) has similar characteristics to its counterpart. In Scotland, special educational needs are governed by the Education (Scotland) Act (1981). Children with more significant difficulties undergo 'recording', a process similar to 'statementing'. Before leaving school children have a future needs assessment instead of a transition plan as used in England and Wales.

Provision for children with learning disabilities
Pre-school services
Children with learning disabilities are referred to child development units run by NHS Trusts. Multidisciplinary assessments are offered with input from, for example, speech and language therapy, clinical psychology, educational psychology, occupational therapy and physiotherapy. Some areas have portage schemes that employ specialist workers to implement structured programmes for children and their families.

Education services
Some educational authorities support children with learning disabilities in a range of special schools. Other authorities are increasingly advocating integration into mainstream schools including pupils with severe disabilities. The nature of integration in practice varies from school to school, and can include specialist units that offer opportunities for social integration, through to full integration where the child with learning disabilities works to an individualised curriculum within the mainstream classroom.

Family support
This is also referred to as short-term breaks (formerly known as respite care). Children spend one or more nights away from the family in a staffed residential service or with another family in a linked scheme. Due to high demand, these services are often under considerable pressure to provide the support needed. Each local authority should maintain a register of disabled children that should influence the planning and provision of services in the area.

Legislation, policy and service provision for adults with learning disabilities

Legislation

NHS and Community Care Act (1990)
This Act has six main objectives:
- to promote a range of services that enable people to live in their own homes wherever possible and appropriate
- to prioritise practical support for carers
- to provide community care-based assessment of individual need
- to work across agencies to provide a comprehensive service
- to establish responsibility and accountability for provision
- to ensure value for money.

Local authorities are under a duty to carry out an assessment of anyone who appears to be in need of community care services, referred to as a **care or needs assessment**.

It is unlikely that the local authority will be able to refuse to carry out an assessment and it should be completed within a reasonable time. The individual's assessed needs will then be considered against eligibility criteria and a range of services may be offered, as part of a care plan. This might include, for example, social work support, home adaptations, meals on wheels, and occupational activities.

The most recent guidance on assessment and eligibility criteria is published by the Department of Health as Fair access to care services (Department of Health, 2002). The guidance states that authorities should operate criteria based on four eligibility bands: critical; substantial; moderate; low. In practice many authorities will only provide services to those whose presenting needs fall within the critical or substantial bands. The whole process of assessment, provision of services and review or reassessment is referred to as 'care management'.

If the person is 'disabled' (ie. blind, deaf or dumb, suffering from mental disorder of any description, handicapped by illness or injury), the local authority must also offer an assessment for services specified in the Chronically Sick and Disabled Persons Act (1970). Guidance advises that services for adults with learning disabilities should be arranged on an individual basis, taking account of *'age, needs, degree of disability, the personal preferences of the individual and his or her parents or carers, culture, race and gender'*.

The local authority is entitled to make reasonable charges for services that they arrange or provide. As an alternative to direct provision of services, a local authority may make direct payments to an individual, which enable the individual to purchase community care services themselves, provided they appear capable of managing a direct payment by themselves or with assistance.

Where care is provided to an individual on a regular but unpaid basis, the carer is also entitled to an assessment of *their* needs under the Carers (Recognition of Services) Act (1995). Direct payments to carers instead of providing services to assist the carer are authorised under the Carers and Disabled Children Act (2000). The most recent legislation on carers, The Carers (Equal Opportunities) Act (2005), requires that local authorities inform carers of their right to an assessment. Carer assessments must take into consideration the carer's wishes about work, education, training or leisure activities, for example, if the carer has a part-time job, arrangements for care during that time should be built into the care plan.

Mental Health Act (1983)

This Act contains powers of compulsory admission and detention in hospital, which may be exercised in limited circumstances when it is in the interest of the person concerned or of wider society, and the mental health difficulties of the patient meet set criteria.

Many of the functions under the Act are given to a specially trained social worker known as an approved social worker. The Act also authorises treatment of a mental disorder and prevents such action being considered false imprisonment and/or assault – even though treatment is without consent in certain circumstances. A person with a learning disability will only be subject to longer-term compulsory measures if in:

> *'a state of arrested or incomplete development of mind which includes severe or significant impairment of intelligence and social functioning and is associated with abnormally aggressive or seriously irresponsible conduct'.*

The Act is supported by a Code of Practice. New mental health legislation has been proposed and is expected in the near future.

Mental incapacity is frequently confused with mental illness and disorder. The issue of mental capacity is crucial in terms of personal autonomy and decision-making. For some people with learning disabilities, capacity to make certain decisions may be limited. This is a complex area and new legislation, the Mental Capacity Act (2005), as recommended by the Law Commission, is due to be fully implemented by October 2007. The Act begins with a number of key principles designed to inform work with people whose capacity may be impaired.

Mental Capacity Act (2005) principles
- People are assumed to have capacity to make decisions.
- A person won't be treated as unable to make a decision until all steps to help him or her have been taken without success.
- A person won't be treated as unable to make a decision just because s/he makes an unwise decision.
- Any acts or decisions for a person who lacks capacity must be in their best interests.

The Act stresses the importance of empowering individuals and enhancing individual decision-making. A person lacks capacity if they are unable to make a decision because of an impairment or disturbance in the functioning of the mind or brain. Being able to make a decision means being able to understand and retain relevant information and use it to make the decision. Capacity will be considered for each individual decision. Many people will be able to make all but the most complex decisions for themselves.

The Act provides a new structure for decision-making for people who lack capacity and includes protection from liability for people, including carers, who act or make decisions on behalf of a person they believe lacks capacity so long as they act in their best interests. A range of new provisions are contained in the Act. A person with capacity may choose someone to act under a lasting power of attorney, in case of future loss of capacity, to make a range of decisions about health, welfare, property and finance. It is also possible, when a person has capacity, to make an advance decision specifying medical treatment the person would not consent to, to apply if the person later lacks capacity.

If a one-off decision needs to be made for a person who lacks capacity to make the decision, the new Court of Protection can make the decision, for example, where the person might live, serious medical treatment or contact with others. If longer-term decision-making is needed the Court can appoint a 'deputy' to do that. In some circumstances where an individual is faced with a major decision, such as a long-term accommodation move, serious medical treatment, or there is an adult protection investigation, an independent mental capacity advocate (IMCA) may be appointed to support and represent the person. The Act also creates a new criminal offence of ill treatment or neglect of a person who lacks capacity. Finally, the Act is supported by a detailed Code of Practice.

Care Standards Act (2000)

This provides the regulation and inspection of residential accommodation and domiciliary services and regulation of the social care workforce.

The Commission for Social Care Inspection (CSCI), which is independent of local or health authorities, undertakes the regulation function and national standards to ensure that all services satisfy minimum levels.

The existence of abuse of adults, including adults with learning disabilities, is clearly established by research and has been recognised in practice and policy. Guidance such as No Secrets (Department of Health, 1999), exists and requires local authorities to have procedures in place to identify and respond to adult abuse, commonly referred to as Adult Protection Guidelines, or Safeguarding Adults. One strategy for preventing abuse is ensuring that unsuitable people do not work closely with vulnerable adults. The Protection of Vulnerable Adults list (POVA) was established under the Care Standards Act. Care providers must refer a person to the list if there are concerns over conduct, which has harmed or placed a vulnerable adult at risk of harm. Providers are also obliged to refer to the list before offering a position of employment. This list will be replaced when new legislation, the Safeguarding Vulnerable Groups Act (2006), is implemented by a new vetting and barring scheme for people who work with children and vulnerable adults.

The Disability Discrimination Acts (1995 and 2000)

This legislation prohibits discrimination against a person with a disability in employment, access and provision of goods and services, and imposes a 'disability equality duty' on public authorities.

A person is discriminated against if s/he is treated less favourably than a person who is not disabled. Disability for these purposes is defined as *'a physical or mental impairment which has a substantial and long term adverse effect on the ability to carry out normal day to day activities'*. A Disability Rights Commission was introduced to support the legislation. The Equality Act (2006) provides for the establishment of a unified Commission, the Commission for Equality and Human Rights, which will supersede the separate commissions for race, sex and disability. Key aspects of the role of the new Commission will be to promote equality and diversity, work towards elimination of discrimination and harassment and enforce the various equality laws.

Human Rights Act (1998)

The Human Rights Act came into force in 2000. It brings the rights and freedoms contained in the European Convention of Human Rights into domestic law.

The effect of the Act is that all laws must be interpreted by the courts so as to comply with the articles of the Convention and it is unlawful for a public authority (including local authorities and the police) to act in a way that is incompatible eg. by denying a person's freedom of expression.

Previously, if a person suffered inhuman or degrading treatment or their right to family life was violated, it may have been necessary to complain to the European Court. The courts in the UK can now deal with such complaints. A number of areas of law have already been found in breach of the Convention, including aspects of the Mental Health Act. It is likely that further breaches will be identified and prompt further law reform. The Act presents an important opportunity to establish a rights-based culture for all members of society.

Policy documents

Before Valuing People (Department of Health, 2001), the two main policy documents addressing the needs of people with learning disabilities were

Health Services for Adults with Learning Disabilities (Department of Health, 1992a) and Social Care for Adults with Learning Disabilities (Department of Health, 1992b). Others include the Mansell Report (Mansell, 1992), which sets an agenda for provision supporting people with challenging behaviour and/or mental health needs, and publications stemming from the Health of the Nation, which raised awareness for the need to support the health of vulnerable groups.

Valuing People is the first government strategy for learning disability produced by the government since the 1971 white paper, Better Services for the Mentally Handicapped. It has four key principles: rights, independence, choice and inclusion. The white paper sets out an agenda for change with an overall objective of addressing the social exclusion of people with learning disabilities. The strategy does not envisage any specific areas of law reform.

Provision for adults with learning disabilities

Any provision should reflect individual choice as far as possible. The support of advocacy services and the principle of empowerment can promote this in reality.

Residential services

About half of all adults with learning disabilities live with their families, while the other half use residential provision. Community care legislation is partly responsible for the expansion of residential services in the private and voluntary sectors. The current models of provision include the following examples.

Village communities

These are managed by the voluntary or private sectors. They tend to have provision for large numbers (over 50 places), often in rural settings, but can be smaller and urban.

Hostels

These are medium sized (10–25 places) and usually run by social services. They can be purpose built or in large converted houses. The number of hostels is currently falling. Research suggests that the quality of support offered is better than in institutions but does not always conform to the principles of ordinary living (eg. Hatton & Emerson, 1996).

Group homes/staffed housing

These are smaller, 'ordinary' houses (two to eight places), historically run by health and social services, but increasingly run by the voluntary sector. Staffed houses can support people with high support needs. The support offered in group homes is generally of a higher quality than that available in larger settings, although there is considerable variance (eg. Hatton & Emerson, 1996).

Supported living

This term is used to describe housing that is based on the principles of separating accommodation from support. Typically, it involves people living alone as named tenants in ordinary flats and houses, but could involve sharing with others. More research is needed to assess the effectiveness of such arrangements.

Specialist residential services

These services aim to support particular characteristics or needs. Examples include: people with challenging behaviour; people at risk of offending; people with multiple disabilities; people with mental health problems. It is likely that this sector is expanding but, again, little evidence has emerged to enable assessment of effectiveness.

Day services

Historically, people with learning disabilities attended purpose-built day centres run by social services, arriving by special transport between normal working hours, Monday to Friday. The appropriateness of these centres has been questioned.

Increases in flexibility mean that adults with learning disabilities can access further education and employment opportunities available to the rest of the population, with individualised support. Accessibility and quality of such arrangements varies greatly geographically, while the complexities of the benefit systems and their impact can affect the ways in which people with learning disabilities get paid for their efforts.

Family and individual support services

Short-break services are also available to adults with learning disabilities and their families, but again, demand tends to outstrip supply. Community-based support from multidisciplinary community teams can contribute to the design of individualised support, but availability and quality is likely to vary according to local issues and resources. For some people, home care or home help may be provided and outreach support can provide a variety of support.

Summary

All supporters of people with learning disabilities need to be familiar – and keep up to date – with the legislative framework in which they work, and the residential and other service options that are available. It is important to ensure that you and your colleagues are informed, and to find ways of passing key points on to the people you support. People with learning disabilities have a right to know just how changes in law and policy will be affecting their daily lives.

Further reading

Brammer A (2006) *Social Work Law (2nd edition).* Harlow: Pearson Education.

Clements L (2004) *Community Care and the Law (3rd edition).* London: Legal Action Group.

Cooper J (Ed) (2000) *Law, Rights and Disability.* London: Jessica Kingsley Publishers.

Read J, Clements L and Ruebain D (2006) *Disabled Children and the Law: Research and good practice (2nd edition).* London: Jessica Kingsley Publishers.

References

Commission for Social Care Inspection (2005) *Social Services Performance Assessment Framework Indicators 2004–2005.* London: CSCI.

Department of Health (1992a) *Health Services for Adults with Learning Disabilities.* London: Department of Health.

Department of Health (1992b) *Social Care for Adults with Learning Disabilities.* London: Department of Health.

Department of Health (1999) *No Secrets: The protection of vulnerable adults – guidance on the development and implementation of multi-agency policies and procedures.* London. Department of Health.

Department of Health (2001) *Valuing People: A new strategy for learning disability for the 21st century.* London: Department of Health.

Department of Health (2002) *Fair Access to Care Services.* London: Department of Health.

Hatton C and Emerson E (1996) *Residential Provision for People with Learning Disabilities: A research review.* Manchester: Hester Adrian Research Centre.

Laming Lord WH (2003) *The Victoria Climbié Inquiry.* London: HMSO.

Mansell JL (1992) *Services for People with Learning Disabilities and Challenging Behaviour or Mental Health Needs: Report of a project group.* London: HMSO.

Jennie Williams
Frank Keating
Zenobia Nadirshaw

Chapter 3

All different, all equal

Anti-oppressive practice and learning disability services

Key words

anti-oppressive practice, discrimination, empowerment practice, equitable, gender-blind, gendered analysis, oppression, social exclusion, social isolation, practitioners, prevalence, punitive, social inequality

Most people recognise that once a person is labelled as having a learning disability they are at risk of social exclusion, disadvantage and discrimination (Department of Health, 2001). What is considerably less well appreciated is the fact that these same people can *also* encounter oppression because of their gender, race, class and sexuality: like everyone else, their lives are shaped by the existence of social inequalities in society. It is against this background that we are going to define anti-oppressive practice, explain why it is needed, and, finally, discuss the implications for action.

Defining anti-oppressive practice

Anti-oppressive practice comprises a set of beliefs, knowledge and practices aimed at reducing the impact of inequality on the lives of service users and sensitivity is needed within service delivery (Di Terlizzi *et al*, 1999).

Oppression operates at different levels that interact to reinforce and sustain such practices (Keating, 1997; Thompson, 1998). Oppression can manifest itself in individual actions, organisational procedures and practices and the ways in which services are organised and delivered. Oppression therefore affects:

- how practitioners behave towards service users
- how people with learning disabilities come to services and the barriers to accessing these
- how services are organised and delivered.

The starting place for anti-oppressive practice is a solid understanding of the many ways that social inequalities can affect both the lives and needs of people with learning disabilities and also how services respond to these needs. Unfortunately, this solid understanding hasn't yet been established within services. This is partly because there is not a great deal of research literature that looks at the implications of social inequalities. It is also because establishing anti-oppressive practice in services can raise both personally and professionally challenging issues to address (Weber, 1998), and good quality training and supervision is not widely available. In the book, *Practising Equality*, Phillipson (1992) observes:

> *'anti-oppressive practice works with a model of empowerment and liberation and requires a fundamental rethinking of values, institutions and relationships'.*

The basis of anti-oppressive practice

We shall focus here on the implications of disability, race and gender. We will look at examples that should help to alert us to the implications of other dimensions of oppression including those based on class, sexuality and age.

Learning disability and oppression

Most people working in services are well aware of the ways that social discrimination and disadvantage can shape the lives of people who are labelled as having a learning disability. Indeed, normalisation theory would not have become so influential without this recognition. People with learning disabilities have been identified as one of the most vulnerable and socially excluded group of individuals in our society. This is highlighted by some of the findings presented in the white paper on learning disability services, Valuing People, (Department of Health, 2001), which pointed out the following examples.

- Families with a child with a learning disability are likely to have higher costs (eg. cases where the child needs support 24 hours a day) and parents may find it difficult to get work because of these added commitments.
- Young people with learning disabilities do not receive adequate support to make the transition to adult life.
- Most people with learning disabilities have little choice and control in their lives.
- Substantial healthcare needs of people with learning disabilities go unmet.
- The number of people with learning disabilities who live in independent housing is relatively small and social isolation remains a problem for people with learning disabilities.

These findings alert us to some of the important ways in which people with learning disabilities are disadvantaged by, and excluded from, society.

Race and ethnicity and oppression

There is no comprehensive research that can help us reliably gauge the incidence and prevalence of learning disabilities across the minority ethnic communities in Britain. There are, however, indications that the prevalence may be higher among some of these communities. For example, the prevalence of learning disability in some South Asian communities has been found to be up to three times greater than in the general population. It would be unwise to try and give meaning to such findings without taking into account the many ways in which people from black and minority ethnic communities experience discrimination in a wide range of areas of their lives.

Examples of such discrimination are that black and minority ethnic communities:

- have higher rates of unemployment than white people (Commission for Racial Equality (CRE), 1997a)
- are over-represented in the criminal justice system (CRE, 1997b)
- are more likely to be excluded from school
- have poorer access to well-paid work, and poorer access to state benefits compared with white counterparts with similar needs (Nadirshaw, 2000).

Building a picture of the possible effects of racial and other inequalities on the life of a person is an essential first step in developing **empowerment practice**. However it is also very important to be aware of the many ways in which inequality can impact on service provision itself. Evidence to date suggests that most services have been uninterested or unsuccessful in taking racial inequality into account, and that racism continues unchallenged within service provision and practice (Baxter *et al*, 1990; Hatton & Emerson, 1999; Nadirshaw, 1999; Reading, 1999). More specifically, Zenobia Nadirshaw (2000) draws attention to evidence that suggests carers often bear the brunt of social exclusion made worse by language barriers and racism, and compounded by negative stereotypes and attitudes.

Carers from ethnic minority communities are often seriously disadvantaged because they lack crucial knowledge about the range of learning disability services that are available, their rights to a community care assessment and how to make a complaint. In addition to this, carers frequently encounter services that underestimate their attachments to cultural traditions and religious beliefs, and are reliant on well-rehearsed stereotypes and generalisations, such as 'they care for their own'. Socio-economic disadvantage and financial insecurity add significantly to carers' experiences of stress, isolation, and marginalisation.

Zenobia Nadirshaw (2000) and others (eg. Di Terlizzi *et al*, 1999) also suggest that people from ethnic minority communities with a learning disability are at a higher risk of being diagnosed as having challenging behaviour, due to stereotyped views and perceptions. They are therefore more likely to be offered more punitive treatments.

Such limitations in service provision to ethnic minority communities are becoming more widely acknowledged. Valuing People (Department of Health, 2001) highlights the fact that the needs of black and minority ethnic people with learning disabilities are different and have to be addressed through the provision of appropriate services.

Gender and oppression

Over the last 30 years there has been increased recognition that gender is a powerful part of our lives and experience. However, people with learning disabilities are often excluded from this debate (McCarthy, 1999). The implications of gender for **women** have attracted the greatest attention from researchers and practitioners.

1 There is evidence from around the world that compared with men, women have less access to resources such as money, status, value, power, leisure, social support and validation (Equal Opportunities Commission (EOC), 2000). We need to know what this means in terms of the lives of women with learning disabilities; the absence of hard evidence shouldn't stop us asking obvious questions.

- Are women and men in our service receiving the same benefits or pay?
- Are women doing more than their fair share of domestic work?
- Is there gender bias in access to services, help, work and leisure?
- Does the equal opportunity policy apply to service users as well as staff?
- Are there opportunities for women in this service to talk together about their lives?
- What equality issues are on the top of their agenda?

2 Inequality and injustice thrive when they are hidden. It is, therefore, reasonable to ask how inequality is hidden or disguised in services.

- Do we blame the victim – those who are most vulnerable and disadvantaged?
- Do we describe behaviour as 'challenging behaviour' (Burns, 2000; Di Terlizzi *et al*, 1999) or 'mental illness' (Downie, 2001) when it would be more appropriate to consider it as a response to the impact or constraints of gender or race?

3 The existence of structural inequalities creates opportunities for very serious abuses of power. Again, there is global evidence that physical and sexual violence and abuse are commonplace, perpetrated overwhelmingly by men. There is a lot of well-developed work on gender in the field of learning disability (eg. Thompson & Brown, 1998; McCarthy, 2000), where there is a very clear recognition of the particular vulnerability of this client group.

4 Gender is the core component of our identity; it gives us a sense of ourselves as male or female. Yet most of the thinking that shapes services is gender-blind, and so too are most of the conversations held about, and with, people with learning disabilities.

Learning disability is the main identity that structures services and interactions. This may make service provision easier but does not help service users in their continuing struggle to assert or define themselves as a woman or a man. However, taking gender into account when working with clients greatly increases the likelihood that we will meet their needs, and also understand how they cope with their difficulties. Michelle McCarthy's work (2000) illustrates the potential of a gendered analysis when working with sexuality. Scior's (2000) study offers a valuable exploration of gender relations and identity as described by women with learning disabilities. Such work lays bare the gender-related tensions, conflicts and losses in their lives.

Finally, there are already well-established attempts to strengthen the collective voice of women with learning disabilities. These include the work of the group Women in Learning Disability (Walmsley, 1997) and the Powerhouse collective (Powerhouse, 1996). People working within the field of learning disability should also borrow enthusiastically and critically from anti-oppressive practice and social action developed elsewhere. This will enable us to identify common threads in our lives and experiences, and to reduce the significance of difference defined by client group membership.

Implications for practice

There are a number of important implications for practice that can be drawn from the information presented here as well as the wider literature on empowerment practice. Empowerment practice is grounded in a well-informed appreciation of the effects of oppression on the lives of clients and their carers, and a familiarity with key concepts such as power, powerlessness, privilege and disadvantage. Acquiring this knowledge is, therefore, a central task. There is a growing literature in the field of learning disability, which can be supplemented by work from other relevant fields including work that focuses on the human and service implications of race and gender inequalities (Fawcett, 2000; Thompson, 1998; Williams, 1999). The challenge for practitioners is that service users may be oppressed on several grounds at the same time (Williams, 2000). Even if a learning disability is the most obvious basis for oppression, it is important to consider whether it is taking place as well, on the grounds of, for example, class, sexuality, age or race.

However, it is not only acquiring this knowledge that is important; workers themselves need to be empowered through supervision and the culture of their workplace to use this knowledge. Empowerment practice is also grounded in a well-informed appreciation of the ways that learning disability services themselves have been shaped by social inequalities. This evidence, which can be gleaned from the research literature, policy papers and from listening carefully to service users and their carers (eg. Atkinson *et al*, 2000), is vital if people working in learning disability services are to challenge, rather than reinforce, social inequalities. This knowledge is essential to providing and developing services that promote rights, independence, choice and inclusion (Department of Health, 2001).

Finally, not only does empowerment practice need to be well informed about the impact of social inequalities on individuals and services, it also needs to be **reflective**. As empowerment practitioners **we need to question** our work continually, as well as the ways in which we try to use our own power in the interests of clients and their carers.

Conclusion

We have a collective and individual responsibility to reduce and eliminate the impact of social inequalities on the lives of people with learning disabilities, their families and carers. Responsibility for action lies with practitioners, service providers and commissioners, trainers and educators, and policy-makers. This action needs to be taken in the knowledge and belief that good care is *not* about treating everyone the same. It is about treating people as unique individuals whose lives and experiences have been shaped by social inequalities.

References

Atkinson D, McCarthy M and Walmsley J (2000) *Good Times, Bad Times: Women with learning disabilities tell their stories.* Kidderminster: BILD.

Baxter C, Poona K and Wad L (1990) *Double Discrimination: Issues and services for people with learning difficulties from black and minority ethnic communities.* London: King's Fund.

Burns J (2000) Gender identity and women with learning disabilities: the third sex. *Clinical Psychology Forum* **137** (March) 11–15.

Commission for Racial Equality (1997a) *CRE Factsheet: Employment and unemployment.* London: CRE.

Commission for Racial Equality (1997b) *CRE Factsheet: Criminal justice in England and Wales.* London: CRE.

Department of Health (2001) *Valuing People: A new strategy for learning disability for the 21st century.* London: Department of Health.

Di Terlizzi M, Cambridge P and Maras P (1999) Gender, ethnicity and challenging behaviour; a literature review and exploratory study. *Tizard Learning Disability Review* **4** (4) 33–44.

Downie S (2001) Falling through the gap. *Feminist Review* **68** (1) 177–180.

Equal Opportunities Commission (2000) *Women and Men in Britain at the Millennium.* Manchester: EOC.

Fawcett B (2000) *Feminist Perspectives on Disability.* Harlow: Prentice Hall.

Hatton C and Emerson E (1999) Commentary: towards equity in service provision. *Tizard Learning Disability Review* **4** (4) 16–19.

Keating F (1997) *Developing an Integrated Approach to Oppression.* London: CCETSW.

McCarthy M (1999) Guest editorial of special issue: Gender matters. *Learning Disability Bulletin* **112** (March) 1–4.

McCarthy M (2000) *Sexuality and Women with Learning Disabilities*. London: Jessica Kingsley Publishers.

Nadirshaw Z (1999) Editorial in special issue: Race, ethnicity and learning disability. *Tizard Learning Disability Review* **4** (4) 2–5.

Nadirshaw Z (2000) Learning disabilities in multicultural Britain. In: D Bhugra and R Cochrane (Eds) *Multi-cultural Psychiatry in Britain*. London: Gaskell Publications.

Phillipson J (1992) *Practising Equality: Women, men and social work*. London: CCETSW.

Powerhouse (1996) Power in the house: women with learning difficulties organising against abuse. In: J Morris *Encounters with Strangers: Feminism and disability*. London: Women's Press.

Reading J (1999) Towards equity in service provision. *Tizard Learning Disability Review* **4** (4) 6–15.

Scior J (2000) Women with disabilities: gendered subjects after all? *Clinical Psychology Forum* **137** (March) 6–10.

Thompson D and Brown H (1998) *Response-ability: Working with men with learning disabilities who have difficult or abusive sexual behaviours*. Brighton: Pavilion Publishing (Brighton) Ltd.

Thompson N (1998) *Promoting Equality: Challenging discrimination and oppression in human services*. Basingstoke: Macmillan.

Walmsley J (1997) Including people with learning difficulties: theory and practice. In: L Barton and M Oliver (Eds) *Disability Studies: Past, present and future.* Leeds: Disability Press.

Weber L (1998) A conceptual framework for understanding race, class, gender, and sexuality. *Psychology of Women Quarterly* **22** (1) 13–32.

Williams J (1999) Social inequalities and mental health. In: C Newness, G Holmes and C Dunn (Eds) *This is Madness: A critical look at psychiatry and the future of mental health services*. Ross-on-Wye: PCCS Books.

Williams J (2000) Endnote from a social inequalities perspective. In: S Baum and J Burns (Eds) Meeting the needs of women with learning disabilities: the significance of gender. *Clinical Psychology Forum* **137** 36–37.

Chapter 4

In safe hands

Protecting people with learning disabilities from abuse

Key words
generic, intermediary, infantilisation, depersonalisation, victimisation, dispossession, responsibility, neglect

Most services for people with learning disabilities now have policies and guidelines on sexual abuse, recognising the vulnerability of people with learning disabilities to sexual abuse and exploitation (eg. Greenwich Social Services, 1993). More recently, generic abuse, adult protection or vulnerable adult policies have been developed, with adult protection at the leading edge of social care policy development. This has been underpinned by a body of research and practice innovation in sexual abuse and learning disability, fuelled by abuse scandals in services for people with learning disabilities in the community. The most renowned of these was known as 'Longcare' (Buckinghamshire County Council, 1998), although fly on-the-wall documentaries have also exposed abuse and mistreatment (Macintyre, 1999). Interestingly, the culture of abuse found in community-based services, such as residential care (Cambridge, 1999) frequently mirrors the characteristics of abuse found in the old long-stay hospitals (Martin, 1984), and indeed more recently the abuse of people with learning disabilities in NHS provisions in Cornwall (CSCI, 2006).

Such has been the prevalence of abuse across the adult client groups that in 2000 the Department of Health published No Secrets, making adult protection a national policy priority. It provided guidance on developing and implementing multi-agency policies and procedures to protect vulnerable adults from abuse. In particular it focused on:

- setting the scene and risk management (what we know using evidence from research)
- suggestions for setting up inter-agency frameworks (multi-agency working, roles and responsibilities, agency and officer lead and operation)
- developing policies and wider strategies (principles, training, commissioning, confidentiality)
- procedures for responding (investigations, record-keeping, disciplinary procedures, advocacy)
- getting the message across (recruitment, guidelines, volunteers, information).

No Secrets required social services departments to co-ordinate local policy and action with heath agencies and the police, as well as other national and local government agencies. For example, the Commission for Social Care Inspection (CSCI) has responsibility for regulating standards in social care provision and often uncovers abuse. Similarly the police need to be involved in cases where criminal offences may have been committed against vulnerable adults, such as rape or neglect leading to death. Indeed, in many authorities the police now have special investigations or vulnerable adult units with specialist officers working on adult protection (Cambridge & Parkes, 2006a). In some adult protection cases, such as those involving clients with care managers or community nurses, there may need to be a joint investigation between social services and health (Cambridge & Parkes, 2006b).

The Protection of Vulnerable Adults (POVA) scheme (Department of Health, 2003) established a list of those who might pose a risk to vulnerable adults, such as workers suspected of abuse. Used alongside police checks, it provides an additional safeguard when appointing people to work with vulnerable adults in social care settings, although, as yet it does not include those working in healthcare. It needs to be remembered that No Secrets is not underpinned by legislation. Being a permissive model, adult protection practice still varies considerably from authority to authority, and across agencies locally. However, there is a general consensus that adult protection is likely to develop into a statutory model similar to that experienced with child protection.

Protecting witnesses within the legal system

Speaking up for justice (Home Office, 1998) reported on the treatment of vulnerable witnesses in the criminal justice system giving evidence in court and made recommendations that were incorporated into the Youth Justice and Criminal Evidence Act (1999) and an implementation programme, Action for Justice (Home Office, 2000). These included special measures designed to assist vulnerable or intimidated witnesses to give evidence as competent witnesses and reduce intimidation and fear:

- the assistance of an intermediary
- signing
- permission to use unsworn evidence
- use of screens and video links
- video recordings of evidence
- clearing the court
- removal of wigs and gowns.

However, despite these measures, the Crown Prosecution Service (CPS) will often fail to support a prosecution in an adult protection case because the chances of success are seen as slim. This is due to the nature of evidence in adult protection cases and considerations of witness reliability. More recently, legislation has been introduced to make it easier to prosecute those who commit sexual offences against someone with a mental disorder that impedes choice – including a learning disability – and as a result is unable to refuse involvement in, or freely consent to, sex. The Sexual Offences Act (2003) has replaced old legislation with a series of new offences, including:

- inciting a person with a mental disorder to engage in sexual activity with another person
- engaging in sexual activity in the presence of a person with a mental disorder
- causing a person with a mental disorder to watch a sexual act or image of one.

The act also makes sex between a service user and a worker an offence, even where consent was freely given, and redefines sex to include acts, such as touching of a sexual nature, even through clothes. Moreover, offences address the use of inducements, threats or deceptions.

What we know

In the 1960s, critical studies (eg. Townsend, 1962: Morris, 1969: Robb, 1967) fuelled widespread disquiet about the role of institutions, including the old mental handicap hospitals, and their associations with abuse. Martin (1984) summarised **institutionalised abuse** as:

- individual callousness and brutality
- low standards and morale
- weak and ineffective leadership
- pilfering by staff
- vindictiveness towards complainants
- the failure of management to concern itself with abuse.

Such observations confirmed the connection between institutionalised care and controlling and punishing regimes made by others (Goffman, 1961), characterised by humiliation, dispossession and exclusion (Foucault, 1977).

Language and abuse

Abusive behaviour has also been attributed to attitudes towards people with learning disabilities (Wolfensberger, 1975). Subhuman language and images result in people being treated as children (**infantilisation**), in our not seeing people as individual or even human (**depersonalisation**) and exercising power over them, in small indeliberate ways, and in more obviously abusive ways (**victimisation**). This is reflected in the tendency to decriminalise offences committed against people with learning disabilities (Sobsey, 1994) in both the language used and the incapacity of the criminal justice system to meet their needs. However, as we have seen, the law is changing in favour of supporting people with learning disabilities, with a new legal language emerging. Decriminalisation by the use of language means using terms such as 'sexual abuse' instead of 'rape', 'restraint' instead of 'assault', 'seclusion' instead of 'imprisonment' or 'sedation' instead of 'poisoning'. Using language in this way can provide 'cover' for those wishing to abuse people with learning disabilities, distracting others from the seriousness of the acts committed.

Abuse and power

Others (Hollins, 1994) have explained abuse by looking at the nature of **dependency relationships**, with the risk of abuse increased by the gaps between user and carer needs, or particular models such as 'carer stress' or 'social learning', where, for example, people are put in situations where their capacity to care properly is limited or they observe abuse and assume that it is acceptable. Others have observed how the risk of abuse is higher in closed care relationships such as in bedrooms (Lee-Treweek, 1994) or in specific care interactions, such as intimate care (Cambridge, 2006; McCarthy & Cambridge, 2006). Relative power and powerlessness therefore frequently emerge as central features of abuse in the relationship between the perpetrator and victim – despite many perpetrators having a low social or economic status. In many cases, abuse of vulnerable adults is also simply related to financial greed, cruelty and pure sadism.

Research

More is known about the incidence and prevalence of sexual abuse than any other form of abuse perpetrated against people with learning disabilities. Research on sexual abuse suggests that self-disclosure is the main source for alerting carers to abuse, and individual case studies suggest that it is critical for facilitating the wider disclosure of abusive regimes. In recognition of this, there have been attempts to familiarise people with learning disabilities with court procedures as well as the legislative changes outlined above. Both men and women with learning disabilities are known to be potential victims of sexual abuse, with the prevalence of sexual abuse ranging from 8–83% of the population of people with learning disabilities, and the incidence of sexual abuse ranging between 0.5 and 4.0 per thousand, depending on the study sample. Men with learning disabilities are also the largest known group of sexual offenders against other people with learning disabilities, followed by staff and family members.

Defining vulnerability and the different types of abuse

Adult vulnerability has been defined by the Law Commission (1995), which states that a vulnerable adult is any person over the age of eighteen who: *'is in need of community care services by reason of mental or other disability, age or illness and who is or may be unable to take care of himself or herself, or unable to protect himself or herself against significant harm or serious exploitation'*. (Law Commission, 1995)

Adult abuse is defined as: *'Physical, sexual, financial, emotional or psychological violation or neglect of a person unable to protect themselves or to prevent from happening or to remove themselves from abuse or potential abuse by others'*. (Law Commission, 1995)

Many agency policies on adult protection define the different categories of abuse and give examples of the signs and signals associated with each type.

In reality however, different types of abuse can also happen in individual cases. **Psychological abuse**, in the form of threats and intimidation, is commonly associated with sexual abuse. **Financial abuse** may accompany sexual or physical abuse. **Discriminatory abuse** such as racism or homophobia often accompanies physical abuse or neglect. No Secrets acknowledges the significance of multiple abuse, both in relation to the different types of abuse perpetrated towards one individual and abuse from a perpetrator towards a number of different victims. Indeed, recent studies on reporting and recording of abuse have highlighted the prominence of multiple abuse (Action on Elder Abuse, 2006; Cambridge *et al*, 2006). The typology of abuse defined and exampled by No Secrets is now central to the categories appearing in local multi-agency policies and covers:

- physical abuse
- sexual abuse
- psychological abuse
- financial or material abuse
- neglect and acts of omission
- discriminatory abuse.

Physical and sexual abuse are invariably prominent, particularly in relation to people with learning disabilities, reflecting both the severity and prevalence of abuse both perpetrated and experienced. However, there are likely to be areas where abuse is relatively hidden and under-reported, such as neglect and financial abuse.

Misuse of guidelines

Neglect is receiving greater prominence, as it is often associated with poor quality services and a failure to provide adequate care. The **breaking of care guidelines** comes under this category, although it is often part of a wider culture of abuse, for example, inappropriate use of control and restraint procedures (physical interventions) in response to violent challenging behaviours (Harris, 1996).

The misuse of control and restraint procedures has received considerable attention in relation to adult protection because these procedures can be harmful (Spreat *et al*, 1986; Williams, 1995) and have received prominence in recent investigations (see *Box 1*).

> ## Box 1: Case study
>
> An influential inquiry into the abuse of people with learning disabilities, known as Longcare (Buckinghamshire County Council, 1998), centred on independent provisions where residents had been systematically abused by the owner, including sexual and physical abuse, having their care and support withdrawn and the misuse of medication.
>
> Social services had continued to purchase from Longcare, despite allegations of abuse, with the inspection and registration service failing to act on the conditions prevailing in the service.
>
> A television exposé of the abuse of people with learning disabilities and challenging behaviours in private care in Medway (Macintyre, 1999) pointed to similar systems failures, although this was smaller scale. Here, for example, physical interventions were misused and people were psychologically and physically abused as a result. The recent inquiry into the abuse of people with learning disabilities in Cornwall (CSCI, 2006) also found systemic failures in care, including poor quality services, financial irregularities, over reliance on medication and poor quality staff training, as well as many instances of abuse.

Other areas of risk in adult protection lie closer to day-to-day practices. Intimate and personal care is an area of work that has also been associated with high-risk situations, particularly as it is often people with profound and multiple disabilities – who are most often excluded – that require help in this area of their lives. It also highlights the tension between privacy and accountability, the importance of consent to touch and communication and consultation with users, and the shortcomings of policies, such as same-gender care. While the latter may protect women with learning disabilities from sexual abuse, such policies leave men with learning disabilities open to this risk and do not address the risks of neglect and physical abuse. Intimate care also often confronts issues of sexuality relating to both staff and service users, as it often requires exposure and touching of intimate and sexual body parts.

What to look for

Organisations and settings

A number of factors are common to abusive cultures in services for people with learning disabilities in the community, and some are similar to those found in the past in hospitals. The following factors have all been linked to abusive regimes (Buckinghamshire County Council, 1998; Cambridge, 1999; Macintyre, 1999):

- closed and inward-looking services and negative staff attitudes
- isolated and secretive organisations and services
- distant management style
- poor or no supervision
- intimidation and threats.

Similar methodologies have been employed for defining the characteristics of potential victims and perpetrators in services for people with learning disabilities (see *Box 2*).

Box 2: Characteristics of victims and perpetrators

Characteristics of victims
- Impaired defences
- Impaired communication
- Compliance
- Low self-image

Characteristics of perpetrators
- The need for control
- Displaced aggression
- Low self-esteem
- Little attachment to victims

Based on Sobsey, 1994

Signs and signals

Using physical abuse as an example, there are particular signs and signals to watch out for in people with learning disabilities, which can alert us to the risk of abuse. These include:

- unexplained injuries or bruises
- increases in the frequency, severity or duration of challenging behaviours
- withdrawal or mood swings
- fear of certain people or places.

Is it abuse?

A useful way to help us think about and define abuse is to consider whether actions or behaviours are *intended* as abusive, at the same time as considering whether actions or behaviours are *experienced* as abusive. *Table 1* summarises a formulation for defining suspected abuse. Unlike some approaches, it acknowledges that there is sometimes a lack of clarity between abuse and consent, and the information we would like, to be able to act decisively in an investigation, is not always available.

Table 1: Deconstructing the boundaries between abuse and consent

Categories of intent and experience	Intended as abusive	Not intended as abusive	Impossible to ascertain intent
Experienced as abusive	Clearly abuse	Probably abuse	Should be treated initially as abuse
Not experienced as abusive	Probably abuse	Clearly not abuse	Probably not abuse
Impossible to ascertain how experienced	Should be treated initially as abuse	Probably not abuse	Impossible to tell whether or not abuse

Cambridge, 2004, developed from McCarthy and Thompson, 1994

Responsibility

Services need to fine-tune the support for clients and staff in responding to abuse, neglect and mistreatment. Often, responsibility has stopped with frontline staff, when there are wider issues of competence that need to be addressed. For example, developing individualised approaches to communication with clients; making high-risk situations or challenging areas of practice visible in recruitment and supervision; developing individual guidelines that tell staff how to support individual clients well, rather than simply listing tasks. A large area of need is for post-abuse work, such as counselling, with people with learning disabilities and the development of men's and women's groups for victims of sexual abuse.

What to do

Most policies and procedures will have clear information on how to report any concerns about abuse and what to do and not to do in particular instances, including action to protect the potential victim and not to alert the potential perpetrator (see AIMS for Adult Protection packs, Brown, 1998; 1999). The different stages in the adult protection process will usually include:

- completing an alert
- reporting your concerns
- a planning meeting for an investigation
- undertaking an investigation

- sharing the findings at a case conference
- monitoring and evaluating progress.

Who is involved in each stage will be determined by the adult protection team, investigator or manager. Sometimes the person's care manager or a specialist adult protection co-ordinator will lead an investigation and sometimes, where there is a criminal aspect to the case, the police will take responsibility. It will be particularly important, for example, that the police lead both video disclosure interviews with victims and interviews with alleged perpetrators. Of course, not all cases will follow the complete process and the process itself may not move through all the steps described, as there could be feedback between the different stages – particularly if the case is complex. Cases often close with no conclusive evidence and without the outcomes that were aimed for or expected.

Adult protection responsibilities will usually rest with a senior manager or community teams or named individuals, such as reporting officers or adult protection co-ordinators. Such procedures are required in order to help ensure that the evidence is effectively managed. Different types of evidence may have different significance and importance and include:

- forensic and medical evidence (the police generally collect this)
- witness disclosures and statements via interviews
- circumstantial evidence (such as staff rotas or information in logs)
- self-disclosure and interviews with victim
- documentary evidence and records (eg. individual care guidelines, policies, service audits etc).

How these types of evidence generally emerge and fit in the investigation process will vary, hence the need for careful planning, management and co-ordination. One particularly important consideration to emerge from various enquiries has been lack of support for staff witnesses who disclose abuse and such measures should be addressed in whistle-blowing policies.

Concluding observations

Services and researchers have come together to look at how adult protection can be taken forward in commissioning services (Brown, 1996) and through functions such as inspection and registration (Brown *et al*, 1996). Consideration has also been given to issues for implementing adult protection policies in local authorities (Brown & Stein, 1998). With generic training materials such as the AIMS for Adult Protection packs (Brown, 1998; 1999), and codes of practice in important specialist areas such as physical interventions, adult protection competence in services for people with learning disabilities is continuing to improve, built on early work in sexual abuse. However, we need to continually improve preventive and early detection work and make sure that the thresholds to reporting abuse and the tolerance of abuse are low. This is sometimes difficult when staff and managers often do not have time for routine responsibilities, let alone taking on additional tasks such as those associated with adult protection, which can bring with them major resource implications.

Guidelines for supporting witnesses who blow the whistle on abuse need to be built into adult protection procedures and adopted by commissioning agencies. Staff and managers on adult protection training universally report a failure to effectively support whistle-blowers, an observation also stemming from inquiries (Cambridge, 1999).

Such policies can:

- minimise the potentially negative emotional and psychological effects on the whistle-blower
- reduce the stress and anxiety related to involvement in subsequent investigations or legal action
- protect the person from negative economic or employment consequences
- give other potential witnesses the encouragement to disclose abuse.

Part of making services safer is making services more open and accountable, both to service users and those who fund them, and this is something that policies alone cannot achieve. Management and practice need to be scrutinised and reviewed in both constructive and empowering ways. Good recruitment practices, support and supervision systems for managers and staff, and training and development strategies are among the more important preventive elements. Kent and Medway Social Services have, for example, developed a common training framework targeted at different levels depending on the roles that staff are expected to play in adult protection (ADSS, 2005).

Most importantly however, service users need access to effective individual planning, advocacy and education on sexuality, rights and assertiveness, and, for those without a voice, individualised approaches to communication. Investment in truly person-centred planning and person-centred ways of working is also needed if we are to combat the social and economic exclusion of people with learning disabilities – enabling them to participate in defining their own care and services. This alone, will reduce the risk of abuse, although the wider implementation of personal budgets will raise new risks such as financial abuse, requiring new checks and balances. Having knowledge, a voice and the confidence to disclose abuse, whether to a client, to staff or a family member, is an example of real empowerment.

Further reading

BILD (2001) *BILD Code of Practice for Trainers in the Use of Physical Interventions*. Kidderminster: BILD.

Brown H, Stein J and Turk V (1995) The sexual abuse of adults with learning disabilities: report of a second two year incidence survey. *Mental Handicap Research* **8** (1) 1–22.

Cambridge P (2001) Managing abuse inquiries: methodology, organisation, process and politics. *Journal of Adult Protection* **3** (3) 6–20.

Sanders A, Creaton J, Bird S and Weber L (1997) *Victims with Learning Disabilities: Negotiating the criminal justice system*. Occasional paper no 17. Oxford: Centre for Criminological Research, University of Oxford.

Wardhaugh J and Wilding P (1993) Towards an explanation of the corruption of care. *Critical Social Policy* **13** (37) 4–31.

References

Action on Elder Abuse (2006) *Adult Protection Data Collection and Reporting Requirements*. London: AEA.

Association of Directors of Social Services (2005) *Safeguarding Adults: A national framework for standards for good practice and outcomes in adult protection work*. London: ADSS.

Brown H (1996) *Towards Safer Commissioning: A handbook for purchasers and commissioners*. Nottingham: NAPSAC.

Brown H (1998) *AIMs for Adult Protection: The alerter's training pack*. Brighton: Pavilion Publishing (Brighton) Ltd.

Brown H (1999) *AIMs for Adult Protection: The investigator's training pack*. Brighton: Pavilion Publishing (Brighton) Ltd.

Brown H, Brammer A, Craft A and McKay C (1996) *Towards Better Safeguards: A handbook for inspectors and registration officers*. Nottingham: NAPSAC.

Brown H and Stein J (1998) Implementing adult protection policies in Kent and East Sussex. *Journal of Social Policy* **27** (3) 371–396.

Buckinghamshire County Council (1998) *Independent Longcare Inquiry*. Buckinghamshire: County Council.

Cambridge P (1999) The first hit: a case study of the physical abuse of people with learning disabilities and challenging behaviours in a residential service. *Disability and Society* **14** (3) 285–308.

Cambridge P (2004) Abuse inquiries as learning tools for social care organisations. In: N Stanley and J Manthorpe *The Age of the Inquiry: Learning and blaming in health and social care*. London: Routledge.

Cambridge P (2006) The case for a new 'case' management in services for people with learning disabilities. *British Journal of Social Work* [advance access published online 31 October 2006].

Cambridge P, Beadle-Brown J, Milne A, Mansell J and Whelton B (2006) *Exploring the Risk Factors, Nature and Monitoring of Adult Protection Alerts*. Canterbury: Tizard Centre.

Cambridge P and Parkes T (2006a) The tension between mainstream competence and specialization in adult protection: an evaluation of the role of the adult protection co-ordinator. *British Journal of Social Work* **36** (2) 299–321.

Cambridge P and Parkes T (2006b) The management and practice of joint adult protection investigations between health and social services: issues arising from a training intervention. *Social Work Education* **25** (8).

Commission for Social Care Inspection (2006) *Joint Investigation into the Provision of Services for People with Learning Disabilities at Cornwall Partnership NHS Trust*. London: CSCI.

Department of Health (2000) *No Secrets: Guidance on developing and implementing multi-agency policies and procedures to protect vulnerable adults from abuse*. London: Department of Health.

Department of Health (2003) *Protection of Vulnerable Adults Scheme: A practical guide*. London: Department of Health.

Foucault M (1977) *Discipline and Punish*. London: Allen Lane.

Goffman E (1961) *Asylums*. New York: Anchor.

Greenwich Social Services (1993) *Recognising and Responding to the Sexual Abuse of Adults with Learning Disabilities*. London: Greenwich Social Services and Greenwich Health Authority.

Harris J (1996) Physical restraint procedures for managing challenging behaviours presented by mentally retarded adults and children. *Research in Developmental Disabilities* **17** 99–134.

Home Office (1998) *Speaking up for Justice: Report of the interdepartmental working group on the treatment of vulnerable or intimidated witnesses in the criminal justice system*. London: Home Office.

Home Office (2000) *Action for Justice*. London: Home Office.

Hollins S (1994) Relationships between perpetrators and victims of physical and sexual abuse. In: J Harris and A Craft (Eds) *People with Learning Disabilities at Risk of Physical or Sexual Abuse*. Seminar papers no 4. Kidderminster: BILD.

Law Commission (1995) *Mental Incapacity*. Report 231. London: HMSO.

Lee-Treweek G (1994) Bedroom abuse: the hidden work in a nursing home. *Generations Review* **4** (1) 2–4.

Macintyre D (1999) *Macintyre Undercover* [Shown on BBC One on 16 November 1999].

Martin J (1984) *Hospitals in Trouble*. Blackwell: Oxford.

McCarthy M and Cambridge P (2006) Sexuality and intimate and personal care. In: S Carnaby and P Cambridge (Eds) *Intimate and Personal Care with People with Learning Disabilities*. London: Jessica Kingsley Publishers.

McCarthy M and Thompson D (1994) *Sex and Staff Training*. Brighton: Pavilion Publishing (Brighton) Ltd.

Morris P (1969) *Put Away*. London: Routledge.

Robb B (1967) *Sans Everything: A case to answer*. London: Nelson.

Sobsey D (1994) *Violence and Abuse in the Lives of People with Learning Disabilities*. London: Brookes.

Spreat S, Lipinski D, Hill J and Halpin M (1986) Safety indices associated with the use of contingent restraint procedures. *Applied Research in Mental Retardation* **7** 475–481.

Townsend P (1962) *The Last Refuge*. London: Routledge.

Williams C (1995) *Invisible Victims: Crime and abuse against people with learning difficulties*. London: Jessica Kingsley Publishers.

Wolfensberger W (1975) *The Origin and Nature of our Institutional Models*. Syracuse: Human Policy Press.

Paul Cambridge

Chapter 5

Taking risks

Assessing and managing risks

Key words

informed risk-taking, risk assessment, risk management, exploitation, consent, policies, policy guidelines

Risk management in services for people with learning disabilities happens along a continuum, from 'informal' risk management to 'formal' risk management. Some things we do automatically, like stopping someone that we know has no understanding of danger from crossing a busy main road on their own (**informal**). Other things we do in a more considered way, such as supporting someone to boil a kettle and make a cup of tea, because this is in their individual plan (**formal**). Occasionally, risk-taking itself is referenced through formal policies that are designed to support staff to assess and manage risks – usually relating to clients. These are not always about reducing risk per se, but about supporting someone to make informed choices in their life and support them through the consequences. However, there is a 'risk' that poorly developed risk management is more about defensive practice than user choice and empowerment. The part that other policies play in risk management is explored later.

Why take risks?

At one time, segregation in institutions was perceived to be the main way of managing the safety and security of people with learning disabilities (Alaszewski *et al*, 1999). However, risk management and risk-taking in community services for people with learning disabilities provides the basis for helping service users to develop their potential as individuals and become more independent. They are also central to some particular areas of practice – such as supporting people with challenging behaviours – and include the risks to the person, other service users or staff. People with learning disabilities often lack the knowledge and experience to take **informed risks** – they may not be aware of exactly what the risk is, or how risky it is. Services therefore, have responsibilities beyond simply providing information or advice to clients.

Keeping records

Risk assessment is designed to identify the level and nature of risk. **Risk management** looks at the more complex relationships between risk-taking and other demands on services, such as the duty of care, responsibilities for protecting vulnerable people and individual rights. It therefore usually leads to an action plan or intervention, with allocated responsibilities.

Such decisions should be part of the service user's individual plan, and be developed from the person-centred plan. They will generally be subject to the approval of managers or the guidance provided by policies. It is important to **record** all risk-taking decisions with the reasons for and against the course of action taken, the rationale for particular decisions made, or risk-management strategy adopted. Being able to demonstrate that decisions involving risk were professionally and responsibly made will not only help to protect the service from claims of negligence, but are also basic to best practice.

In this chapter, intimate and personal care is used to explore how carefully policies need to be formulated to avoid hidden risks. HIV is used as a worked example to consider the issues inherent in risk assessment and risk management, the processes involved and the different approaches that staff and services can take.

Basic risk management

Risk-taking is directly related to participation in life and taking up opportunities to develop as individuals, whatever an individual's level of learning disability. It would therefore be unrealistic to try to achieve a risk-free life for service users. Some lifestyle risks, such as those associated with smoking or diet, are increasingly being recognised as important for supporting clients, and reflect national health promotion initiatives. Much will depend on what is made visible and said about risk-taking in regular policies and guidelines, individual plans and, occasionally, specific risk-taking policies. Risk management has its roots in cost-benefit analysis, and has been more prominent in health than social care (Eby, 2000).

A basic model for risk management and decision-making in social care will usually include the following criteria or actions (developed from Carson, 1990).

- Draw up lists of competing considerations ('pros' and 'cons') regarding the risk (benefits and costs) to the client.
- Do the same for the staff or service (advantages and disadvantages).
- Consider both the length of the respective lists as well as the relative importance and weighting of the different factors.
- Identify who is responsible for making the decision and what model of decision-making is best (single worker, team, senior manager, director, specialist adviser).
- Consider the frequency of likely occurrence of the risk events (how often they might happen).
- Identify any action that could be taken to reduce uncertainty.
- Consider the steps that could be taken to make the benefits or advantages more likely to occur.
- Consider long-term gains and risks against short-term gains and risks.
- Record the decisions made and responsibilities for the actions recommended.

Although the Jay Committee (Jay, 1979) and Social Services Inspectorate (Fruin, 1998) both stressed the importance of risk-taking and related policies, Alaszewski *et al* (1999) also observed that only a small minority of agencies surveyed had risk or whistle-blowing policies. Key findings from their study also highlighted the different perceptions of risk on the part of service users, relatives and professionals, with the conclusion that effective risk policies should comprise:

- a clear statement of aims and the purpose of the policy
- a clear definition of risk, identifying issues, consequences and probability
- a clear statement of components, including planning and assessment, and decision-making
- recording a clear statement of policy and practice for risk management.

The role of policies in risk management

There are critical areas of practice where risk and policy merge. Some policies and procedures, such as those on infection control, are specifically designed to reduce or minimise a particular risk to staff and clients. Policies on control and restraint (physical interventions) are designed to ensure that agreed individual procedures are adhered to when responding to challenging behaviours, which should minimise risks of abuse and harm to clients (Harris *et al*, 1996; Harris, 2002). In other policies, such those on sexuality, risk management is likely to be referenced in relation to particular issues, such as HIV and sexual abuse (Cambridge & McCarthy, 1997). As can be seen in *Chapter 4*, adult protection policies are largely about assessing, managing and responding to risk in a specific area of national and local policy. They are designed to guide managers and practitioners through procedures that allocate responsibilities, and specify processes to follow and decisions to make, with the aims, for example, of keeping clients safe and removing perpetrators. Therefore, risk and risk management in services for people with learning disabilities are also affected by how well policies are developed, implemented and reviewed, and staff skills and training (Brown & Cambridge, 1997). To be effective, policies should link risk management with key practice issues such as decision-making and accountability (O'Sullivan, 1999; Cambridge & Parkes, 2004; Eby, 2000) (see *Box 1*).

HIV risk assessment

Without knowing the nature or level of risk, it cannot be effectively managed. In relation to HIV, we know the main ways HIV can be transmitted, providing the basic information we need to undertake HIV risk assessment.

Most HIV infections are transmitted through infected blood, semen or vaginal fluid. Therefore, the main potential and actual routes of infection are through:

- high HIV-risk sex (unprotected anal or vaginal sex, either as the insertive or receptive partner) with a person infected with HIV
- sharing needles for intravenous drug use (rather than using new, clean needles each time drugs are injected)
- medical procedures using contaminated blood, blood products or tissue (screening or treatment has now eliminated this in the developed world)
- vertical transmission from mother to child during pregnancy or childbirth.

Box 1: Policy case study

As with other policies, those on intimate and personal care are designed to improve practice and the quality of care provided to service users, yet may also unwittingly ignore or bring additional risks. Therefore, it is important to review policies regularly to ensure that they are as effective as possible. In intimate and personal care for example (Cambridge, 2006), most policies will be based on same-gender care due to the fact that intimate care may involve washing or bathing someone or changing continence pads. This is because of the perceived risks to female clients of sexual abuse from male carers and the cultural inappropriateness of cross-gender care from men to women. However, sometimes this is given priority, in order to keep to the policy, resulting in a service user receiving intimate care from agency staff who do not know them or understand their care needs. This may lead to assumptions that intimate and personal care is best conducted by women – regardless of the gender of the client. In reality, women are often expected to provide intimate care to men because, in general, fewer men than women work in frontline caring roles. Lesbian and gay staff might also be placed in a difficult position by same-gender policies. A categorical approach to gender may distract attention from other risks, such as sexual abuse towards men, as well as the high risks of physical abuse and neglect from care interactions, which are conducted in private and closed settings. However, on the positive side, good intimate and personal care policies will refer to individual care guidelines, which support care to be delivered in appropriate and consistent ways, outlining how to respond appropriately and safely if someone gets sexually aroused during a care interaction and how to communicate effectively with a client who has limited expressive or receptive communication. For example, exploring consent to touch and explaining reasons for touch.

In reality, we will need to know much more to undertake an effective HIV risk assessment in a particular risk area, such as sexuality. For example, detailed consideration would include recognising that:

- using a condom for penetrative anal or vaginal sex reduces, but does not eliminate, the risk of HIV infection – condoms can split or come off during penetrative sex and the use of water-based lubricants and extra strong condoms for anal sex can help prevent this from happening
- the receptive partner is at more risk than the insertive partner
- anal sex is higher risk than vaginal sex
- oral sex is generally considered as very much safer than unprotected penetrative sex, even without the use of condoms, unless semen is exchanged or blood is present.

In Britain, most known cases of Aids and HIV infections are accounted for by men, the majority of whom have had sex with other men. Heterosexual transmission and infections accounted for by women are steadily increasing, and infections accounted for by intravenous drug use and contaminated blood products/tissue are decreasing proportionately. HIV risk is also related to global factors, such as the high incidence of HIV infection among people in parts of Africa, south east Asia and eastern Europe. Clearly, we would need to know a lot about someone's sexual life and encounters in order to undertake an effective HIV risk assessment, as key factors would include:

- type of sex (high risk if anal or vaginal penetrative sex, low risk if oral sex)
- whether condoms are used regularly and effectively (safer penetrative sex)
- frequency of unsafe sexual behaviours (the more frequent, the more risk of HIV)
- the risk group of the sexual partner (potentially higher if with men who have sex with men, people from Africa or intravenous drug users who share needles, for example)
- sex and safer sex education (knowledge of sex and safer sex)
- ability to practise safer sex (including assertiveness and negotiating skills)
- reported realities of sexual encounters (from keyworking or sex education).

In addition, **indirect indicators of risk** might need to be used to help assess the likelihood that sex and high HIV-risk sex might be taking place. For example, for men with learning disabilities who have sex with men without learning disabilities (Cambridge, 1996), various things might indicate that someone may be at increased risk, such as:

- being seen hanging around public toilets, parks or other places that men meet to have sex
- talking about homosexuality or gay sex
- having a gay identity
- talking about friendships with other men
- being absent from the service for long periods without explanation
- having unexplained money or presents
- having an unexplained sexually transmitted infection
- being secretive or refusing to talk about activities.

The majority of men with learning disabilities at risk of HIV are also likely to be having sex with other men and women with learning disabilities

(Cambridge, 1996; 1997a), raising additional considerations for HIV risk assessment and management.

HIV risk management

HIV infection is potentially a much less likely risk than sexual abuse (the prevalence of sexual abuse is known to be high: Brown *et al*, 1995; McCarthy & Thompson, 1997). However, it is potentially a more serious risk, because life is invariably at stake and there are major social and economic costs, such as quality of life and drug treatments. HIV is also an easy risk to ignore, as high HIV-risk behaviours may be invisible (such as unsafe sex outside services), the consequences may be longer-term (long timescales between HIV infection and illness) and the difficulties in attributing specific events to infection. Individual rights to sexual activity and opportunities for sexual expression have to be judged in relation to the risks involved for the person and others. Such considerations make HIV risk management decisions difficult.

Drawing a bold line between acceptable and unacceptable HIV risk is impossible, as people attach different values and benefits to risk-taking. However, services can ask some basic questions about people's understanding and appreciation of sex, safer sex and HIV. This helps to assess informed risk-taking and the nature of possible HIV preventive (risk management) activities (Cambridge, 1997b).

- Is the contact mutual or exploitative? If it is exploitative there is a clear case for intervening to stop it, regardless of HIV risk.
- Is the behaviour high risk? If someone is having unprotected anal or vaginal sex there is clearly a significant risk to be managed, whereas oral sex or other sexual contact could be assessed as low risk – requiring a lower priority intervention.
- Is the behaviour frequent or likely to reoccur? A one-off medium- to high-risk event is likely to require a very different response from a situation of repeated risk-taking, which is likely to continue.
- Does the person at risk know about safer sex and are they physically able to practise it? If not they should receive intensive safer sex education, have access to condoms and receive ongoing staff support and monitoring.
- Is the person at risk able to insist on safer sex and that they or their partner(s) use condoms for high HIV-risk activities, such as penetrative anal or vaginal sex? If not, then they should receive HIV counselling, intensive safer sex education and training for assertiveness and negotiating skills.

Most responses will involve safer sex education and assertiveness work (Cambridge, 1999), but in some cases risk will be so high, or knowledge so low, that short- or long-term measures might need to be taken to restrict or eliminate high HIV-risk behaviours. However, such decisions need to take account of rights and responsibilities at both the individual client and service levels. *Table 1* illustrates an increasingly complex level of decision-taking and risk management in relation to HIV, for an individual case. Similarly, the potential legal risks for services will increase as the level of risk increases (Gunn, 1997).

Conclusions

In summary, a number of possible HIV risk management responses can be identified:

- testing for HIV (see below)
- keeping someone at home
- escorting someone when out
- limiting someone's activities when at home
- providing safer sex education
- counselling for HIV
- referral to specialist GUM service
- referral to gay men's support/advocacy group.

The potential responses vary in their approach and acceptability and have various advantages and disadvantages, which will need to be considered on an individual basis. Simply encouraging a gay identity will not, for example, be a preferred option for many men with learning disabilities, who have sex with men who usually retain a heterosexual identity (Cambridge, 1997a). The evidence from sex education suggests a wide gap between the knowledge and practice of safer sex, for people with learning disabilities (McCarthy & Thompson, 1998). Restricting someone's activities might infringe their liberty or lead to an increase in challenging behaviour.

HIV testing is potentially a very important part of HIV risk assessment and risk management. If an HIV test is thought necessary, then it may only legally be done if the individual can give informed consent to it. Without informed consent, an HIV test amounts to assault. To give informed consent (as opposed to saying yes) a person must not be encouraged, or otherwise pressured, to have the test, and must appreciate the potential consequences and limitations (Cambridge, 1997c).

**Table 1: Decision-making for HIV risk assessment and risk management –
example of a sexually active male client**

Level of decision	Examples of level of risk	Examples of decision taking
1	Change in known sexual behaviour raises possible sexual health issues	Keyworker or support worker informs house manager and care manager
	Need for safer sex education discussed as part of individual person planning	
2	Referral for client to have safer sex education	House manager consults with service manager, with advice from sexuality co-ordinator
	HIV risk assessment undertaken	
	Decision not to involve parents in discussion of client's sexuality at request of client	
3	High HIV risk disclosed/assessed (client sometimes has unprotected insertive or receptive anal sex with men without learning disabilities)	Service manager informs operations manager, with advice from sexuality co-ordinator
	Assertiveness programme designed to help client negotiate and practise safer sex (basic HIV risk management)	
	Safer sex education continued, counselling regarding HIV risk and consequences, and messages reinforced and targeted at known high HIV-risk behaviours	
4	Further disclosures through sex education that client sometimes has sex with other men and women with learning disabilities	Meeting between house, service and operations managers and sexuality co-ordinator
	Decision to provide others with individual sex and safer sex education	
	Local HIV risk management strategy developed	
5	Client requests HIV test and referred to specialist counselling GUM (genito-urinary medicine, ie. sexual health) clinic	Operations manager, with advice from sexuality co-ordinator and ethical committee or independent adviser
	HIV risk management programmes for individual clients at risk are established	

In particular they should:

- understand the nature of HIV/Aids
- appreciate the nature and limits of the HIV test
- be able to demonstrate why they want a test
- be able to consider confidentiality and disclosure
- appreciate the emotional and social consequences of testing positive or negative.

Testing for HIV

Only people with mild learning disabilities are likely to be able to give such informed consent. If a test is considered without the individual's informed consent, this must be legally sanctioned by a court of law. Moreover, counselling would need to be provided, and protocols for managing confidentiality would need to be in place (Cambridge, 2001). However, the rationale for testing is strong, as known HIV-positive status can bring access to effective combination drug therapies and healthcare monitoring. Dedicated HIV policies and the inclusion of sexual health issues in sexuality policies are needed to guide service responses and risk management in this area of practice, with safer sex education available for all sexually active clients. This should be targeted at men with learning disabilities who have sex with men, and women with learning disabilities who sell sex, or have many men without learning disabilities as sexual partners (Cambridge, 1999).

Policies and practice

At a more general level, risk management policies and procedures can help, but these need to be accessible and practical for service managers and staff to use effectively. One way of achieving this is for risk management to be fully placed within specific policies that relate to the area of practice. For example, risks that relate to HIV can be addressed through sexuality policies (Cambridge & McCarthy, 1997) or specific HIV policies (Horizon, 1996).

Summary

Guidelines for risk management in services for people with learning disabilities need to empower staff and managers to take positive risks in relation to supporting service users in routine things (such as developing life skills) and complex things (such as increasing their independence and participating in the community).

The following checklist should help to achieve an operational relationship between promoting individual rights and protecting people from danger – and enable services to develop a positive culture of risk-taking. For every risk situation it is important to think about the following points:

- the potential benefits or gains to the person's functioning, quality of life and life experience *as well* as the risks to the person and the service
- the costs, to services and staff *as well* as to service users, of perpetuating institutionalised dependency relationships through a reluctance to take risks
- the learning and mutual respect that can be developed *between staff and service users* from supporting positive risk-taking in people's lives
- the risks of developing a culture of introspection (ie. self-scrutiny) through excessively defensive management and practice.

Every risk, whether routine and low level (such as boiling a kettle), or higher level (such as road safety and HIV) can be addressed through a basic risk assessment in a person's individual plan, with actions and responsibilities made clear. However, not all risk-taking will necessarily have positive outcomes – otherwise it would not be risk-taking. The outcome is to minimise risk and maximise gain. In so doing, we also need to consider the support that both staff and service users may need if risk-taking goes wrong. Learning from negative, as well as positive, outcomes of risk-taking can happen at case review and service review, but only if we do not develop a culture of blame and fault. More importantly, good policies and procedures should support risk-taking in key areas of practice. *Chapter 4* provides a worked example of adult protection and *Box 1* (page 55) shows how a policy focusing on a particular area of practice, such as intimate and personal care, can help with effective risk management. Increasingly, service-providing agencies are developing specific risk management policies and procedures, but we need to make sure that they work well for service users, as well as managers and practitioners.

Further reading

McCarthy M (1997) HIV and heterosexual sex. In: P Cambridge and H Brown (Eds) *HIV and Learning Disability*. Kidderminster: BILD.

Thompson D (1997) Safer sex work with men with learning disabilities who have sex with men. In: P Cambridge and H Brown (Eds) *HIV and Learning Disability*. Kidderminster: BILD.

References

Alaszewski H, Parker A and Alaszewski A (1999) *Empowerment and Protection: The development of policies and practices in risk assessment and risk management in services for people with learning disabilities*. London: Mental Health Foundation.

Brown H and Cambridge P (1997) Policies and their contribution to coherent decision-making. In: P Cambridge and H Brown (Eds) *HIV and Learning Disability*. Kidderminster: BILD.

Brown H, Stein J and Turk V (1995) The sexual abuse of adults with learning disabilities: report of a second two year incidence survey. *Mental Handicap Research* **8** (1) 1–22.

Cambridge P (1996) Men with learning disabilities who have sex with men in public places: mapping the needs of services and users in South East London. *Journal of Intellectual Disability Research* **40** (3) 241–251.

Cambridge P (1997a) How far to gay?: the politics of HIV in learning disability. *Disability and Society* **12** (3) 427–453.

Cambridge P (1997b) At whose risk? Priorities and conflicts for policy development in HIV and intellectual disability. *Journal of Applied Research in Intellectual Disability* **10** (2) 83–104.

Cambridge P (1997c) *HIV, Sex and Learning Disability*. Brighton: Pavilion Publishing (Brighton) Ltd.

Cambridge P (1999) Considerations for informing safer sex education work with men with learning disabilities. *British Journal of Learning Disabilities* **27** (4) 123–126.

Cambridge P (2001) The HIV testing of a man with learning disabilities: informed consent, confidentiality and policy. *The Journal of Adult Protection* **3** (4) 23–28.

Cambridge P (2006) Developing policies, procedures and guidelines for intimate and personal care in services for people with learning disabilities. In S Carnaby and P Cambridge (Eds) *Intimate and Personal Care with People with Learning Disabilities*. London: Jessica Kingsley Publishers.

Cambridge P and McCarthy M (1997) Developing and implementing sexuality policy for a learning disability provider service. *Health and Social Care in the Community* **5** (4) 227–236.

Cambridge P and Parkes T (2004) Good enough decision-making? Improving decision-making in adult protection. *Social Work Education* **23** (6) 711–729.

Carson D (1990) Taking risks with patients – your assessment strategy. In: *Professional Nurse: The staff nurse's survival guide* pp83–87. London: Austen Cornish.

Eby M (2000) The challenges of being accountable. In: A Brechin, H Brown and M Eby (Eds) (2000) *Critical Practice in Health and Social Care*. London: Sage.

Fruin D (1998) *Moving into the Mainstream: The report of a national inspection of services for adults with learning disabilities*. London: Department of Health.

Gunn M (1997) The law, HIV and people with learning disabilities. In: P Cambridge and H Brown (Eds) *HIV and Learning Disability*. Kidderminster: BILD.

Harris J (2002) From good intentions to improved practice – developing effective policies. In: D Allen (Ed) *Ethical Approaches to Physical Interventions*. Kidderminster: BILD.

Harris J, Allen D, Cornick M, Jefferson A and Mills R (1996) *Physical Intervention: A policy framework*. Kidderminster: BILD.

Horizon (1996) *Policy on HIV Infection and Testing for People with Learning Disabilities*. Abbots Langley: Horizon NHS Trust.

Jay P (1979) *Report of the Committee of Enquiry into Mental Handicap Nursing and Care*. London: HMSO.

McCarthy M and Thompson D (1997) A prevalence study of sexual abuse of adults with intellectual disability referred for sex education. *Journal of Applied Research in Intellectual Disability* **10** (2) 105–124.

McCarthy M and Thompson D (1998) *Sex and the 3Rs: Rights, responsibilities and risks*. Brighton: Pavilion Publishing (Brighton) Ltd.

O'Sullivan T (1999) *Decision-making in Social Work*. London: Palgrave.

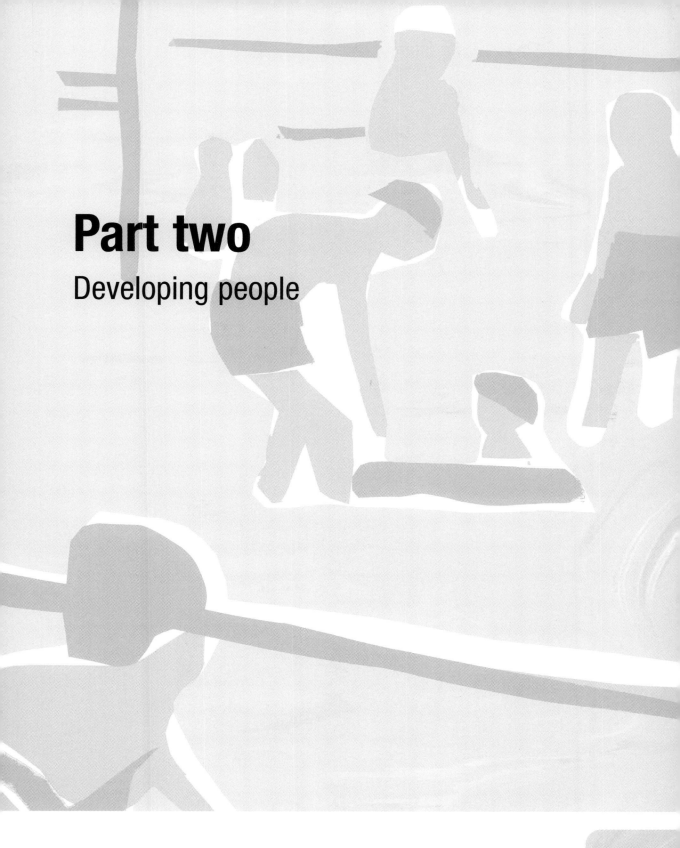

Part two

Developing people

Chapter 6

Between you and me

Developing communication in partnership with people with learning disabilities

Key words
partnership, communication environment, sensory loss, developing staff skills, alternative and augmentative communication

Many people with learning disabilities will experience some level of difficulty in engaging in successful acts of communication. This may be because of the nature of the learning disability or associated disabilities (such as sensory or physical disabilities). It is also likely to be influenced by other people (for example, whether they provide opportunities to communicate) and the environment (including the nature of the setting). This chapter describes some of the communication difficulties that people with learning disabilities are likely to experience and suggests ways that these difficulties can be minimised.

Prevalence

Communication difficulties are common among people with learning disabilities, though the estimates depend on the methods used. In the total population it is estimated that around 4.3% of people have communication difficulties, whereas studies of people with learning disabilities have found that as many as 89% needed speech and language therapy intervention, and that at least 45% of people with learning disabilities experience serious problems with communication. In general, people with more severe learning disabilities are likely to have more difficulties in communicating. Difficulties can be seen within all areas of communication. Some of these difficulties are listed in *Table 1*.

Table 1: Possible difficulties in communication and people with learning disabilities

Type of communication difficulty	Example
Expressive skills	Having only one or two words or signs
	Difficulties in speaking clearly meaning that speech is hard to understand
	Being unable to use any formal communication (such as words, signs or symbols) and having to rely on the interpretations made by other people
Understanding skills	Difficulties understanding complex sentence structure
	Needing support from the context
	Only understanding key words
Functional, social interaction or pragmatic skills	Difficulties using communication in a functional way, for example to request items Finding it hard to take part in a conversation
	Interpreting language literally
	People with autistic spectrum disorders often have particular problems with this area of communication

Sensory loss

Hearing loss is also associated with level of learning disability. Studies have shown that around 40% of adults with a learning disability have a hearing loss that is severe enough to need intervention. Research has found that hearing loss is also likely to increase with age. Having a hearing loss makes understanding and using spoken information more difficult. This depends on the nature and extent of the loss. For example, some types of hearing loss mean that all sounds are heard at a reduced volume (conductive loss) meaning that raising the volume of spoken communication may be helpful. However, if the person has a sensorineural hearing loss, the sounds of speech may become distorted and simply raising the volume of speech will not be adequate.

There is evidence to suggest that staff teams who work with people with learning disabilities do not always have the skills to recognise a hearing loss and so may not realise that someone they are working with is having difficulties hearing. Ideally, everyone should have access to high-quality hearing assessments. There are a range of assessments, depending on the skills and abilities of the person who is being assessed.

In terms of other disabilities, it is apparent that visual loss affects a similar proportion of people with learning disabilities as hearing loss. Research has shown that prevalence of hearing loss, visual loss and dual sensory impairment increases with severity of learning disability, with the highest rates occurring among people with profound learning disabilities. Though the impact of these additional disabilities is difficult to quantify, they are likely to be multiple, and will make taking part (in communication, activities and the community) even more difficult.

Box 1 shows a summary of issues relating to sensory loss and people with learning disabilities.

Box 1: Sensory loss and people with learning disabilities
- 40% of people with learning disabilities have a significant hearing loss
- Hearing loss increases with age
- Staff teams often do not recognise hearing loss
- 40% of people with learning disabilities have a visual loss
- People with more severe learning disabilities are more likely to have some form of sensory loss

Difficulties interpreting communication

People with learning disabilities who have severe communication difficulties may need to rely on other people to interpret their communications. They may be very limited in their use of formal communication (such as using words, signs or symbols). Studies have demonstrated that the ways in which people communicate can be quite inconsistent and this can mean that it is not always easy to work out what the person might mean.

Research has shown that people with learning disabilities are also more likely to say yes to questions, even if they have not understood what you are asking them. This may be because they do not want to create difficulties. People often find it very difficult to let you know that they have not understood, or to let you know if you have made a mistake in interpreting their communication. This all makes the person with a learning disability particularly vulnerable. The See What I Mean (SWIM) guidelines (Grove *et al*, 2000) were developed to help in situations where it is difficult to work out what someone may want.

Box 2 contains a summary of issues relating to difficulties interpreting communication.

Box 2: Difficulties interpreting communication in people with learning disabilities

- All communication involves some degree of interpretation but people with severe communication difficulties may be more reliant on other people's interpretations
- People may have inconsistent ways of communicating
- People may be more likely to say yes, even if they have not understood the question

---

Multi-modal communication

In reality, most communication is multi-modal and involves a variety of different ways of communicating. For example, someone may use speech as their main way of interacting, but may also use gesture and facial expression. The use of alternative and augmentative communication (AAC) is common in people with learning disabilities.

Some of the different forms of AAC are shown in *Table 2*. These can be used in different ways to help communication, depending on the needs of the person with a learning disability. For example, a person with a learning disability might select appropriate symbols to show that they are hungry. Alternatively, other people may use signs, symbols or objects to ask the person with a learning disability if they would like some lunch.

Difficulties understanding communication

Many people with learning disabilities have difficulties in understanding communication; they may find it difficult to understand spoken communication and rely on the context and situation in order to work out what is happening and what is expected of them. People may need additional support from signed communication, symbols or objects of reference to help them to understand the words that are being used. People may have good understanding of the words being used (such as words that refer to emotions, time and negatives). People may generally

Table 2: AAC and people with learning disabilities

Form of communication	Example
Objects of reference	Objects are used to represent an item or event. For example, a cup might be used to represent a drink, or a piece of swimming costume material may be used to represent swimming
Symbols or photographs	Symbols can be used in place of written words to make text more accessible to people. Alternatively, they may be used by the person with a learning disability to make their needs known. These include: Rebus, Makaton, PCS and Compic
Signed communication	Key word signing, such as Makaton, sign languages, such as British Sign Language and speech-based systems, such as Paget Gorman Sign System
Voice output communication aids (VOCA)	Possible messages are stored on the communication aid for the person to access. For example, the person may press the symbol 'help' to activate the spoken message that they need help

have a good understanding but have difficulties with more complicated sentence structures (such as the use of passive sentences).

Research has shown that staff may find it difficult to work out how much people with learning disabilities understand. One study found that less than 20% of staff questioned mentioned that the service users they worked with had difficulties in understanding communication. It seems that staff often think that people can understand more than assessments show and that this is more likely in conversational settings. Communicating in a way that the person finds difficult to understand may result in unrealistic opportunities to participate in communication exchanges, making it more difficult for the person to develop their communication skills.

Staff may find it difficult to adapt their communication to the understanding skills of the person they are talking to because they misunderstand service philosophies; staff recognise the importance of normalisation and social role valorisation but think that this also means normalising communication and therefore talking as they would talk to anyone. Alternatively, staff may find it difficult to simplify their language and use an adult style of interaction at the same time. They may, therefore, use a more complex style of interaction as it feels more appropriate when talking to an adult.

An understanding of other people's communication is usually supported by the context and situation in which the communicative act occurs. This may mean that very little understanding of the words used is necessary. In some situations it may be very clear what is expected from the person from what is happening in the environment. This is often the case where actions are part of a routine.

For example, saying to someone *'Can you get the milk out of the fridge now please?'*, may seem like a complex sentence but if this request is made at the end of the process of making a cup of tea, when getting the milk is always the next step, the person may not need to understand any of the words used. Rather, the request is carried out because the person is able to understand that this is the next step in the routine and is what is most likely to be being asked.

It can be difficult to work out what information the person understands from what is being said, and what information they understand from the context and situation. If staff do not recognise that service users are getting information from the context and situation, they may assume that they are understanding the spoken words and therefore, that the service user is able to understand quite complex spoken information. This could create problems when they are trying to communicate with service users without this contextual support and use complicated language that the service user is not able to understand.

A summary of issues relating to difficulties in understanding can be found in *Box 3*.

Communication environments

Services should provide support that is adapted to meet individual communication skills and needs. This involves recognising the individual's communication abilities and then adapting communication so that it is appropriate to the person's skills. The amount of communication between staff and service users is important, as environments where high-quality communication occurs frequently are likely to encourage and develop communication skills. However, research has also shown that service users are often supported in situations where communication occurs infrequently. In addition, the communication that does take place often seems to be of a short duration and low quality.

Box 3: Difficulties understanding communication

- People with learning disabilities often find it difficult to understand what is being communicated
- People often rely on their knowledge of the context and situation to help them to understand what is expected
- People often find it easier to understand words that relate to objects, people, places or events
- Understanding words that relate to abstract concepts such as time or emotions is often more difficult
- Using a complicated sentence structure makes understanding more difficult
- Staff often overestimate people's understanding skills and think that they understand more than they can

Some types of communication are more likely to initiate conversations, such as comments and questions. The evidence seems to show that the sort of communication acts that take place with people with learning disabilities are less likely to encourage responses. Studies have also shown that staff are more likely to use verbal communication, even if service users are communicating using signs and symbols.

A summary of issues relating to communication environments can be found in *Box 4*.

Box 4: Communication environments

- Service users are often supported in poor communication environments – services need to ensure that they meet communication needs
- Communication often occurs infrequently
- Communication is often too complex for people to understand
- Staff communication does not always provide people with opportunities to respond
- Staff usually use verbal communication, even if service users are communicating with signs or symbols

Strategies to help communication

It is important to remember that attitudes and expectations will influence the communication exchange. For example, if a member of staff believes that someone with learning disabilities is unable to communicate, or contribute to their person-centred planning process, they are unlikely to offer them opportunities to take part. If someone with a learning disability has learnt that their attempts to communicate are often missed (which can happen in busy and chaotic environments) they may not feel motivated to continue to try and express themselves. There are a number of helpful communication strategies that can aid communication.

Communication priorities within services

There are many different ways of supporting communication skills. Some of these involve thinking about communication across the services in which people are supported. For example, The City and Hackney Learning Difficulties Service are clearly working towards considering service user communication skills in all areas of their service. In their mission statement, the team state:

> *'The effort and time commitment involved in supporting someone's communication needs to be seen as a priority for the whole service in order for us to become truly "person centred" and that everyone has the right to be given the opportunity to try out and access different and new systems of communication in order to achieve this.*

> *'Anything impacting on people's lives should be communicated to them in a way that they understand. People have a right to be involved in their own reviews, and communication needs to be adapted to suit the individual to facilitate this.'*

In this policy, the importance of everyone using a variety of methods of communication (eg. signs, symbols and objects in addition to verbal communication) is stressed.

Some other examples of service strategies can be seen in **Box 5**.

Staff communication

Other communication strategies are more concerned with changing the ways that communication partners interact with service users.

> *'A communication partnership involves two or more people who exchange ideas and interpret meanings.'* (Bartlett & Bunning, 1997)

Box 5: Communication strategies across the service

- Using a total communication strategy across the service, where a variety of methods are used in meaningful ways
- Developing a resource of signs, symbols, photographs etc to be used
- Introducing accessible communication passports for service users and communication books for staff, which contain key information, including a description of how people are able to communicate, their likes and dislikes etc
- Making sure that all service users have a communication profile that describes and illustrates their communication strengths and needs
- Staff training in communication strategies

Ideally, partners should adapt their communication to each person's communication needs. *Table 3* (overleaf) gives examples of some of the ways that staff may adapt their communication.

Other communication strategies involve ways of helping the person to develop their communication skills. Your local speech and language therapy service will be able to provide information on relevant strategies. Communication occurs in partnership; so using the strategies described in *Table 3* should have a positive impact on communication skills. Positive experiences of taking part in successful communication exchanges will also have an important impact. Some of these strategies can be seen in *Table 4* (overleaf).

Summary

Research has shown that the most effective strategies are those that involve a combination of the approaches listed in this chapter. Services need to highlight the importance of communication and have a service-wide strategy that aims to support and develop communication. Communication involves a partnership between those involved, and therefore works best when considering both the person with a learning disability and their communication partners, and targeting the skills of all those involved.

Table 3: Communication partner strategies

Strategy	Example
Making sure the person can see and hear to the best of their ability	Making use of natural light and making sure that you are not in shadow as you speak
	Ensuring that if the person wears hearing aids or glasses that they are using them (and, in the case of hearing aids, that they are working properly)
Ensuring that the person is comfortable	Making sure that the person is not too hot or cold
	Ensuring that the environment is not too noisy or full of distractions
Making sure you gain the person's attention before you start communicating (this is particularly important for people with additional sensory difficulties)	You might touch the person on their arm or hand
	For someone with dual sensory loss you could identify yourself with a particular tactile marker (such as a bracelet with a particular pattern on) so the person knows who you are
Keeping language simple andclear	Communicating one message at a time, in the simplest way possible
Using support from the environment	Communicating what is happening, when it is happening
	Using objects, symbols or photographs to illustrate what you are communicating
Using a variety of different communication methods	Using additional gestures, signs or pictures – this is particularly important if someone has difficulties in understanding
	Using additional communication supports if you are communicating with someone who uses them is very important, as it shows that you value their ways of communicating
Making sure that the person has their communication supports available	Making sure that the person has any symbols or photographs that they use to communicate with them
Giving the person time to respond and making sure you react to all their communication signals	Ensuring that you respond to subtle signals such as changes in facial expression

Table 3: *continued*

Strategy	Example
Checking that they have understood your communication and that you have understood theirs	Checking with other people that they agree with your interpretation
	Telling the person what you think they are communicating (being aware that they may find it difficult to let you know if you have got it wrong)
	Keeping a record of their responses over time

Table 4: Strategies that can help the person with a learning disability to develop their skills

Strategy	Example
Giving the person other ways of communicating	Supporting the person to use objects or symbols
Developing communicative signals	Making sure other people respond consistently to communicative signals. If everyone disagrees about what signals mean, it is very difficult for the person to develop their skills
Introducing new vocabulary	Does the person need to be able to communicate something new? (This chosen item should be within the person's understanding skills and be something that they will be motivated to use and have plenty of opportunity to apply)
Developing interaction skills	Introducing strategies to repair communication breakdown

Further reading

Ambalu S (1997) Communication. In: J O'Hara and Sperlinger A (Eds) *Adults with Learning Disabilities*. London: John Wiley and Sons.

Bradshaw J (1998) Assessing and intervening in the communication environment. *British Journal of Learning Disabilities* **26** 62–66.

Foundation for People with Learning Disabilities (2000) *Choice Discovered*. London: FPLD.

Grove N and McIntosh B (2002) *Communication for Person Centred Planning*. London: City University and King's College.

References

Bartlett C and Bunning K (1997) The importance of communication partnerships: a study to investigate the communicative exchanges between staff and adults with learning disabilities. *British Journal of Learning Disabilities* **25** 148–153.

Grove N, Bunning K, Porter J and Morgan M (2000) *See What I Mean: Guidelines to aid understanding of communication by people with severe and profound learning disabilities*. Kidderminster: BILD/Mencap.

Steven Carnaby
Claudia Linton
Julie Roberts

Chapter 7

Making plans

Undertaking assessment and person-centred planning

Key words

person-centred, assessment, evaluation, planning, implementation

We often take the day-to-day running of our lives for granted. Some of the things we do are almost automatic – getting out of bed in the morning, getting dressed, finding the cereal packet – while other activities, such as going on holiday, are likely to need more thought. This process of thinking about what we want or need to do involves weighing up the situation (*'Where do I want to go on holiday?'*, *'How long shall I go for?'*), and then some planning as to how things will happen (*'I'll cancel the milk, book a taxi to the airport and order some travellers' cheques'*).

People with learning disabilities are no different. They also need to assess the situation and plan before they act, and might need help to do this. In addition, it is possible that the *range* of activities needing assessment and planning will be greater, as people with learning disabilities often need some degree of support to get on with their lives. Indeed, using the example above, individuals with greater levels of disability might need a careful process of assessment and planning to help them to get out of bed and have breakfast, as well as for going on holiday.

'Good' support for people with learning disabilities needs careful planning if it is to meet an individual's needs appropriately and, therefore, skills in assessment and care planning are central to developing quality services. This chapter defines the assessment and care planning process, and suggests key elements for best practice in this important area.

Why are assessment and care planning so important?

Assessment and care planning form half of what can be described as *'the basic helping cycle'* (Taylor & Devine, 1993), the other elements being implementation and evaluation. In practice, these four stages can be thought of as:

- **Assessment:** What is the problem? What needs to be learnt? What are the strengths and limitations in this situation?
- **Planning**: What should be done about it? By whom?
- **Implementation:** Let's get into action!
- **Evaluation**: How are things at the end of our efforts?

It is useful to think of these elements as a cycle that is theoretically continuous (see *Figure 1*).

Figure 1: The 'basic helping cycle'
(adapted from Taylor & Devine, 1993)

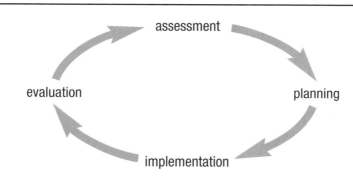

assessment

planning

implementation

evaluation

Assessment and planning are crucial – without these stages, the supporter is likely to 'dive in' and support the individual with learning disabilities without thinking about important aspects, such as:

- potential risks
- the extent and nature of what is needed
- how to be sure that the support provided is effective in meeting the individual's needs
- most importantly, how to ensure the individual is fully involved in whatever is decided.

What is meant by 'assessment'?

Assessment is the process by which needs are identified – an aid for planning support or intervention. The characteristics of assessment are listed in *Box 1*.

Box 1: Key characteristics of assessment

- Gathering information about the situation from as many sources as possible, but particularly from the perspective of the individual with learning disabilities
- Identifying potential areas for development or change as well as areas of strength and resourcefulness in the individual
- Placing the information gathered within specific relevant contexts eg. frameworks relating to legislation, service policy, culture and ethnicity
- Identifying potential obstacles to any future work that may be carried out
- Establishing the level of existing strengths and needs as a baseline by which to measure progress of any future intervention
- Building strong rapport between the individual with learning disabilities and the individual(s) offering support, to encourage an open working relationship

---

When using any assessment process, it is important to be clear about its **aims**. In practice this will mean that you need to:

1 establish the reason for undertaking the assessment
2 be clear about who will act on the information provided by the assessment
3 set out clear, specific questions that you hope to answer using the information gathered by the assessment.

In other words, before undertaking an assessment of any kind, you should be able to answer the questions listed in *Box 2*. If any of the answers to those questions are not straightforward, there is a good chance that you need to think more carefully about the type of assessment you have chosen.

Box 2: Pre-assessment checklist

- Why is this question being asked?
- How will the information gathered be used?
- Who will use the information?
- Are the results of the assessment likely to be of practical benefit to the individual with learning disabilities?

The process of assessment

The precise nature of any assessment will clearly be directly linked with the individual, his or her situation and the issue(s) being addressed. However, assessments should always be:

- **reliable** – they could be repeated and similar outcomes would be achieved
- **efficient** – the outcome is worth the effort made
- **valid** – they give an accurate picture of what is happening
- **useful** – they fulfil a purpose.

The assessment process can be divided into the two main phases of:

1 gathering information
2 analysing information.

Gathering information

Information can be obtained in a variety of ways, including observation, interviewing the service user and his/her family, and using written sources. The precise strategy to adopt depends on both the nature of the issue being addressed and the abilities and characteristics of the individual with learning disabilities that you are supporting. The process will need to be adapted accordingly. For example, if the individual does not communicate in standard ways, your assessment could include creative techniques for ensuring that his/her perspective remains central to your findings. Such techniques may include using video to record how the person shows likes and dislikes, or supporting him/her to use a diary with photographs of activities.

Interviewing individuals with learning disabilities as part of your assessment

Where the individual can be interviewed more conventionally it is important that, as an interviewer, you are aware of the difficulties that have the potential to affect the information that you are recording. A wide body of research has suggested that interviews with people who have learning disabilities need to be conducted with a range of issues in mind. These are listed in *Box 3*.

Conducting observation

It may be helpful to conduct observations across a variety of settings and situations with the individual, alone and in a group. Observations should be planned and carried out with the individual's consent wherever possible, or with consent gained from significant others. It is important to record what you observe as objectively as possible, being aware of the context in which

Box 3: Issues in interviewing people with learning disabilities (adapted from Ambalu, 1997)

- Explain the purpose of the interview
- If you are not familiar with the person, find out from carers or relatives the best way to communicate with him/her
- Use short, simple sentences
- Speak slowly
- Pause after each sentence
- Avoid the use of jargon
- After making a statement ask the person to tell you what you have said to check what they have understood
- Use the person's communication aid(s) where appropriate
- Break explanations down into steps and use photographs and/or drawings, if possible
- Use open questions (for example, 'tell me about…')
- Avoid using questions that require a yes/no answer
- Be aware of difficulties in understanding time and number concepts (for example, 'before' and 'after')
- If the person's speech is difficult to understand, do not pretend you have understood. Ask him or her to say it again, more slowly, in different words or show you what s/he means
- Watch the person carefully to check that s/he is not becoming distressed
- Remember that parents' or carers' views may differ from those of the person with learning disabilities
- Sum up at the end of the session what will happen next

the events are occurring. Devise individualised recording sheets that capture the breadth and depth of information required.

Figure 2 shows an example of a simple observation sheet for recording incidences of challenging behaviour.

Figure 2: Example of recording sheet used during observation

Date and setting	What happened before the incident? (Who was around? What was the person doing?)	Describe the incident (Give as much detail as possible)	How did staff respond? (What did they say? What did they do?)

Other sources of information

Quite often, your assessment will form part of a wider multidisciplinary assessment, involving a range of professionals. It is essential that information is co-ordinated effectively through regular liaison. Sometimes, community team members, such as clinical psychologists and speech and language therapists, will conduct standardised assessments designed to assess specific abilities or phenomena.

For example, the Wechsler Adult Intelligence Scale (Wechsler, 1997) provides an assessment of an individual's cognitive abilities, while the Pre-Verbal Communication Scale (PVCS) establishes the individual's communication skills. Data gathered during interviews and observation provides invaluable context for the findings derived from these more standardised approaches.

Analysing information

The process of care planning

During assessment, information about the individual with learning disabilities and some aspect of his/her life is recorded and classified in some way. This information is analysed using experience, knowledge and values, as well as that of other colleagues, and considered in the light of evidence from relevant research. Once a clear picture has been developed, planning for how to address the issue(s) can begin.

As with the assessment phase, it is essential that care planning is conducted *with*, and not just for, the individual with learning disabilities (and his/her family where appropriate). Care planning can be considered in terms of issues relating to the individual with learning disabilities and their family, issues concerning support staff, and issues that relate to the wider support organisation. It is important that care planning remains person-centred in its approach and does not let organisational concerns and priorities detract from the individual's involvement in decision-making.

Care plans can relate to a specific issue (eg. intimate care or support with eating) or describe the ways in which an individual's lifestyle is supported more generally (eg. planning a move away from the family home or to more independent accommodation). Whatever the nature or purpose of the care plan, the essential characteristic must be that it is person-centred, both in the process of its creation and during its implementation.

So what is actually meant by being 'person-centred' in the way that we work with people?

Taking a person-centred approach

The government white paper, Valuing People, advocates the use of person-centred planning (PCP) as the backbone of effective provision for people with learning disabilities:

> 'A person-centred approach to planning means that planning should start with the individual (not with services) and take account of their wishes and aspirations. Person-centred planning is a mechanism for reflecting the needs and preferences of a person with a learning disability and covers such issues as housing, education, employment and leisure.' (Department of Health, 2001)

Person-centred planning is an approach to organising assistance to people. Its development can be traced over 30 years in the USA, gaining prominence in Britain because of Valuing People. It is a 'family' of approaches and techniques that share certain characteristics, listed in *Box 4*.

Box 4: Characteristics of person-centred planning
Plans are person-centred if they:
- aim to consider aspirations and capacities rather than needs and deficiencies
- include the individual's social network
- emphasise the provision of support required versus what services can manage.

Person-centred planning also helps to ensure that any planned provision is culturally sensitive and personally relevant. Thinking carefully about the individual's perspective and personal experience will take into account the most appropriate ways in which to assess their needs and organise their care. The approach taken needs to fully adopt the principles of anti-oppressive practice, comprising a set of beliefs, knowledge, and practices aimed at reducing the impact of inequality on the lives of service users (Di Terlizzi *et al*, 1999).

The person-centred planning debate

Person-centred 'planning' and its impact continue to be a matter of debate. For some, there is concern that individual planning systems don't really 'work' anyway (in terms of meaningful inclusion) and risk being little more than a paper exercise. The planning process might not always be well connected to the 'real life' of service users and longer-term goals are often omitted. Most importantly, service users are not always involved in planning their lives in personally relevant ways. There is currently no legal mandate for person-centred planning, and resource constraints and inadequate staff training can lead to half-hearted attempts at carrying things through.

However, those 'hopeful' for its success (eg. Towell & Sanderson, 2004) suggest that individualisation is central to any modern approach to improving the quality of life of people with learning disabilities, and that person-centred planning has learnt from the past by starting with the experiences and aspirations of the individual. They go on to suggest that person-centred planning affirms the need for shifting power in the direction of people using services and flag up the importance of investment in guidance, training, mentoring and networking.

Mansell and Beadle-Brown (2004) stress the value of 'person-centred action' suggesting an attitude towards working with people with learning disabilities that moves way beyond any specific planning system. Some of their suggestions are shown in *Box 5*.

Box 5: Suggestions for taking 'person-centred action' (from Beadle-Brown *et al*, 2005)

- Provide mechanisms for challenging decisions about how resources are allocated
- Provide evidence that implementation makes a difference
- Focus on what really happens in the lives of service users
- Improve the capacity of staff and others to give skilled, facilitative support

The structure of care planning

The term 'care planning' will mean slightly different things according to the organisation in which you work. Care plans can refer to daily support plans that provide details of how the person needs to be supported in daily activities (sometimes called 'support plans'), or can provide a much broader picture of the specific aspects of provision that combine to create a 'care package'. These are planning 'systems' that are given various names (for example, essential lifestyle planning; pathways; life planning) but they all aim to implement the ideology of a service organisation and support an individual to live as independently as possible and fulfil their potential in the community. The important issue here is consistency of terminology and approach.

Main elements

Any care plan, whatever its scope, is likely to have the following elements.

- **Aims and objectives** (What are you and the individual trying to do and why?)
- **Methods** (How will you and the individual carry out the aims and objectives?)
- **Resources** (Who else will help? What materials, equipment or facilities might be needed?)
- **Timescale** (How long will the plan take to put into practice? Will it be broken down into smaller steps?)
- **Monitoring method** (How will you and the individual record what has been achieved?)
- **Evaluation method** (How will you know when stages of the plan have been achieved?)

The plan needs to be written down, but in ways that are primarily meaningful to the individual with learning disabilities. As with the assessment process, it is important to be creative and think laterally. Care plans can be recorded using video, photographs, symbols and signs, audiotape, drawings and information technology.

Reviewing the plan

An equally vital stage of care and support planning is its review. This can be done in meetings involving people who have contributed to the plan's implementation. Again, involving the individual with learning disabilities must remain central. Historically, people with learning disabilities have been largely **excluded** from decision-making in *their* lives, and any attempts at care planning need to avoid inappropriate meetings that are led by professionals and serve the needs of the organisation before the needs of the individual and his or her family. **Good practice involves starting with the person and his or her ways of communication, and finding ways of integrating the person's views with concerns that the service may have regarding important issues, such as risk management and adult protection.**

Case study 1: Staying in touch – Debbie's story

Debbie talked a lot about wanting to see Auntie Polly's grave. She would mention this to her housemates when they had family visiting them. Debbie's supporter, Julie, did some research by looking in old records and asked Debbie more questions about Auntie Polly. Debbie showed Julie a picture in a frame in her bedroom and explained that attempts had been made to look for Auntie Polly before.

Debbie's records from a previous home indicated that she had visited the cemetery with her keyworker, but had been unable to find Auntie Polly's plot. Debbie was understandably very disappointed. Julie asked Debbie if it was a good idea to

telephone one of her relatives to find out more about Auntie Polly, and Debbie agreed.

Julie then spoke to Debbie's cousin and was able to find out more about what had happened to Auntie Polly, eventually planning a meeting at the cemetery on Auntie Polly's birthday so that Debbie could be shown the plot.

Despite Julie's reassurances, Debbie was still convinced that it wasn't going to happen – she'd been let down before. To help allay Debbie's anxiety, Julie worked with Debbie to write down the agreed arrangements and mark the event on her calendar.

This was the start of Debbie's annual visits to Auntie Polly's grave, supported by her family, and staff where she lived. She took pictures of the flowers as well as the train journey. While Debbie looked forward to going to the cemetery, she also began building stronger relationships with the rest of her family.

Case study 2: Going to hospital – Sandra's story

Sandra told people that she was having problems with her eyesight. She went for an eye test, but the opticians were unable to establish what was happening. Sandra had another eye test, this time at the Great Western Eye Hospital in London. The specialists there used coloured images of objects and found that Sandra had cataracts in both eyes.

Sandra became very emotional and frustrated as her sight declined. A circle of support was created around her and Sandra chose staff from the team who support her at home – her keyworker, Julie, another member of staff, Alfie, and the staff team manger, Molly – to be its core members.

continued

Case study 2: continued

There was a lot of talking about the treatment process, visits to various places in the hospital and meetings with the consultants. Julie used her judgment and decided not to take pictures, instead talking to Sandra to about what was happening to lessen her anxiety. Each member of the support circle used the same words with Sandra, as well as role plays, demonstrations and other activities, to increase her awareness and understanding of what was going to happen. The approach used was recorded carefully to enable the repetition of the same techniques to increase familiarity and develop Sandra's confidence.

When the time came, Sandra planned and packed what she would be taking with her: dressing gown, pillowcase, her favourite cuddly toy, a pair of slippers and favourite magazines. At a later date these items were used as objects of reference (see ***Chapter 6***), again to increase familiarity. Sandra was now able to relate and demonstrate what was going to happen by herself.

Alfie supported Sandra to the hospital appointment. During the wait they were able to recite together what was going to happen and read through Sandra's favourite

magazines. Julie arrived later and, as Sandra was still waiting for her appointment, repeated what Alfie had instigated. Sandra was very calm until she saw the plastic covering for shoes and the gown that she would need to wear. She refused to go in. Alfie encouraged her to put them on by putting them on himself, explaining that it was needed or they couldn't go in with her. With gentle encouragement Sandra eventually put hers on too. Later, Molly was there to support Sandra to go home after the operation.

Six months later, Sandra had an operation on her other eye. The same process was used and there was less anxiety for everybody. Julie had also ensured that the same consultant operated on both occasions.

There are moments when Sandra talks about this experience, when *Casualty* or *Holby City* is on the television, or when she looks at the wrist band from the hospital. Her keyworker admits that there were times when she thought 'What if this doesn't happen?' asking herself 'Did we work hard enough to support Sandra?' She also acknowledges that, although the operations were successful, Sandra still talks about it, and the aftermath is equally important. Sandra and Julie will be doing further work by returning to the hospital, this time taking pictures to create a collage or album as a way of supporting Sandra to more fully understand, and come to terms with, what has happened.

Case study 3: Planning in personal context – Huma and Sondonia's story

Sondonia had been working with Huma, who is married to a man who does not have a learning disability. English is a second language for both Huma and her husband. Huma was making some choices around sport activities that she would like to do as a way of meeting other people and keeping fit after having a baby. Sondonia, as her link worker, found out information about suitable places, but realised that they were in an area that Huma's husband was unhappy about Huma visiting. Sondonia was aware that Huma wanted to try things out. She also respected Huma's cultural beliefs, but sensed that Huma's choices were being greatly influenced by those of her husband and family.

There was a period of time when Huma no longer telephoned Sondonia to arrange to meet up for chats. Sondonia had left a few messages, but had no response. She decided to wait a bit longer before trying to contact again.

Huma finally made contact, arranging a meeting time at her own home. When Sondonia arrived Huma's husband refused her entry. This happened many times, and Sondonia became frustrated. Later on Huma had telephoned Sondonia, stating that she had changed her mind and that the couple were refusing support.

Sondonia was frustrated because she at least wanted Huma to have a 'taster' of being supported using a person-centred approach. She concluded that Huma's family perceived Huma's role differently and that Huma herself was somewhat 'caught' between two different cultures. Sondonia also felt that Huma's husband was also trying to protect Huma and was, perhaps, unsure about Sondonia's role in his wife's life, despite attempts to provide clear explanations for him.

Sondonia hopes that in the future, Huma, her husband and family will be able to trust Sondonia enough to invite her back into their lives and work with them again.

Summary: Good practice in assessment and care planning

This chapter has attempted to describe the main characteristics of assessment and person-centred care and support planning and suggested some ideas for good practice. *Box 4* provides a summary checklist.

Box 4: Checklist for good practice in assessment and care planning

- Start with the person and keep him or her at the centre of any assessment, planning or decision-making process
- Consider the issue(s) you are addressing within the wider context of the individual's lifestyle and cultural background
- Collaboration is essential – with the individual, with his or her social network and with other professionals in your organisation
- Always base your assessment and planning on evidence from research
- Be creative with how you support the individual with learning disabilities to express their views
- Keep clear, concise records – and think carefully about who needs to know the outcomes of your assessment. Maintain confidentiality
- Review the care plan regularly
- Avoid making the individual feel as though s/he is living in a laboratory – remember that, in the complexities of charts, guidelines and observations, there lies a human being who should be respected and treated with dignity

Further reading

Cambridge P and Carnaby S (Eds) (2005) *Person Centred Planning and Care Management with People with Learning Disabilities*. London: Jessica Kingsley Publishers.

Circles Network: www.circlesnetwork.org.uk

Paradigm: www.paradigm-uk.org

Foundation for People with Learning Disabilities: www.learningdisabilities.org.uk

Helen Sanderson Associates: www.helensandersonassociates.co.uk

Ask Mencap: www.askmencap.info

References

Ambalu S (1997) Communication. In: J O'Hara and A Sperlinger (Eds) *Adults with Learning Disabilities: A practical approach for health professionals*. Chichester: Wiley Press.

Department of Health (2001) *Valuing People: A new strategy for learning disability for the 21st century*. London: The Stationery Office.

Di Terlizzi M, Cambridge P and Maras P (1999) Gender, ethnicity and challenging behaviour; a literature review and exploratory study. *Tizard Learning Disability Review* **4** (4) 33–44.

Mansell J and Beadle-Brown J (2004) Person-centred planning or person-centred action? A response to the commentaries. *Journal of Applied Research in Intellectual Disabilities* **17** (1) 31–35.

Mansell J, Beadle-Brown J, Ashman B and Ockenden J (2005) *Person-centred Active Support.* Brighton: Pavilion Publishing (Brighton) Ltd.

Taylor B and Devine T (1993) *Assessing Needs and Planning Care in Social Work.* Aldershot: Arena.

Towell D and Sanderson H (2004) Person-centred planning in its strategic context: reframing the Mansell/Beadle-Brown critique. *Journal of Applied Research in Intellectual Disabilities* **17** (1) 17–21.

Wechsler D (1997) *Wechsler Adult Intelligence Scale (3rd edition).* San Antonio: Harcourt Brace and Company.

Chapter 8

Whose life is it anyway?

Handling information and keeping records

Key words

accuracy and appropriateness, confidentiality, communication, duty of care, data protection, negligence, ownership of information, service-user involvement

In this, the information age, many of us would still rather 'have a go' than follow instructions, or do something else, rather than record what we've just done. Surely it's better, I hear you say, that we spend more time with the people we're supporting and less time in the office reading and writing in files. These are natural instincts and, most of the time, will do no harm. However, 'most of the time' is not good enough. Imagine you're receiving care in hospital and the nurse does not read your file (which is stamped clearly with *'allergic to penicillin'*) and, by administering penicillin in accordance with the doctor's instructions (who also hasn't read your file), induces a severe allergic reaction. Such staff would be negligent and would have no defence against your complaint. Similarly, if you, by not reading something you should have read, or by not keeping an accurate record, cause harm to a person with learning disabilities, you are negligent in your duty of care. We may get away with it when we're assembling a new piece of furniture, but the use and accurate recording of information is not optional when we're working with people.

This is particularly crucial in work with people with learning disabilities. If you are conscious enough to see the nurse approaching you with a syringe, you may be able to ask what's in it. In a similar situation, many people with learning disabilities will not be able to do this or will not understand the implications of the answer (see *Box 1*, overleaf).

> ## Box 1: Why we need to keep records
> *'This perspective inevitably leads to a concern with the procedures used for "remembering" the lives of people who cannot remember them for themselves. Since services cannot rely on the service user to tell them about the past and, partly because of staff turnover, cannot count on the memory of the staff, they need to provide a prosthetic memory through regular information collection… Record keeping, while undoubtedly often a boring chore, may need to assume a new importance as a method of helping to achieve personal and cultural continuity.'* (Mansell *et al*, 2001)

In this chapter I will consider:

- what information should be recorded
- how the information should be recorded – so that it is accurate and easily understood by those who need to use it
- how the information should be stored so that it is both secure and accessible
- the importance of confidentiality
- the legal context of data protection
- how we can ensure as much service user involvement as possible, including, where necessary, by the use of 'translation' services.

As an example I will use the context of handling information about an individual's behaviour. There are, of course, many other contexts in which the recording and use of information is crucial, including assessment and care planning, reviewing strategies for intimate and personal care, financial records and other administration.

What information?

Scepticism about the value of recording is often justified. In many services, far too much irrelevant information is recorded (and never used) so that staff can easily begin to feel that all recording is a waste of time. The first principle of handling information, therefore, is **not to create unnecessary information**. Records are much more likely to be kept (and used) if they have a **clear rationale** and can be completed quickly and easily. *Box 2* shows the example of Mrs E to illustrate this.

What should we record here? First, we need to establish why we are recording. There are a number of possible reasons:

Box 2: Mrs E

Mrs E was 70 and living in a house, with three others, supported by a small team of staff 24 hours a day (including sleep-in at night). She was an able lady, who had spent a considerable period of time in a long-stay hospital, having been admitted at a time when it was enough to show unusual behaviour coupled with a difficulty in learning to read and write. Over the last few months her behaviour had become a cause for concern. She would often get up at night and stand at the top of the stairs, shouting about how her brother was dead. This usually woke up the member of staff and the other residents of the house, and it would often take some time to calm her down and for everyone to get back to sleep. Mrs E's brother was not dead and she spoke to him regularly on the phone.

- we may want Mrs E to see a psychiatrist or psychologist, and think it will be helpful if we can say what has been happening, how often and how long it takes her to settle down
- we may feel that having sleep-in cover is no longer sufficient for Mrs E, and want to make a case to managers for temporarily having waking night staff
- we may want to help Mrs E by checking out possible reasons for her getting upset and by checking out what strategies help her to calm down quickly.

Different reasons ought to lead to different recording strategies. We might decide that all these reasons are important and that we will seek to record the following:
- the time that Mrs E gets up and starts shouting
- what she shouts about
- the time that she stops shouting and goes back to bed
- how long the sleep-in member of staff was awake (not just managing the situation, but also recording it!)
- whether other residents were disturbed, and for how long
- whether anything happened the previous evening that might have upset Mrs E – we might already have suspicions about this and, if so, would seek to record this more specifically (eg. whether Mrs E had spoken to her brother on the phone).

It's worth remembering again why this kind of recording is likely to be necessary. If, and when, Mrs E sees a psychiatrist they are likely to want to know how long this has been happening for and how often. Even with her relatively good communication skills, Mrs E may not be able to say. If she is accompanied by a member of staff, that person may have some information but, without systematic recording, they will only be able to give a very partial account – what's happened on the one night a week when they have been sleeping in. Thus, Mrs E is disadvantaged either by the psychiatrist making a decision on the basis of incomplete information, or by delaying a decision until such information is gathered.

How to record

The most common means of recording information is through some kind of diary, in which staff (and occasionally service users) write a narrative account of what has happened. Imagine such a diary entry for Mrs E:

> *'Up all night again with Mrs E screaming and shouting. Mrs D got a bit upset too because she couldn't get back to sleep. I can't cope with this much longer – is anyone doing anything?'*

I expect we've all seen diary entries like this, though, of course, we've never made them ourselves! Diaries have many problems, for example:

- they often fail to separate fact from opinion
- they are often inaccurate (what does 'up all night' mean?)
- they often miss out important information (what was Mrs E shouting about?).

Such records are also very difficult to use. As the diary builds up over days and weeks, the amount of information grows to the point where it would take someone a considerable amount of time to 'mine' it for what is really important eg. how many nights has Mrs E been upset and, on average, for how long?

Often, therefore, a more structured approach to record keeping will be better. Such records are usually much easier for staff to keep (they involve mainly ticking boxes rather than writing at length) and they are much, much easier to use and summarise, for example the member of staff coming in the next day can see at a glance what sort of a night Mrs E and the others have had. In Mrs E's case, a record form along the lines of *Table 1* might be used.

Table 1: A sample recording form

Night	Start time	What did Mrs E do? (eg. she shouted about her brother being dead)	Stop time	What helped to calm her down? (eg. I talked quietly to her)	Were other residents disturbed?	Did anything upset Mrs E? (eg. her brother didn't phone previous evening)
Monday						
Tuesday						
Wednesday						
Thursday						
Friday						

Storing and retrieving information

There's nothing worse than spending a lot of time recording information and then not being able to find it when you need it. This happens to us all, of course – recording is second only to filing in many people's list of pet hates. But, if you can't find it, you can't use it, and you really have wasted your time. Worse, if you can't find it, that might mean it's been left somewhere it shouldn't have been (like on the dining room table) and is currently being read by someone who shouldn't read it. So storage of information is a vital part of the recording process – making sure that the information can be accessed by those who need it, and only by those who need it. There are many different solutions to the storage/filing problem and it would not be appropriate to prescribe particular approaches here. Whatever system you do use should meet the following criteria:

- it's easy for you to put information in it
- it's easy for appropriate others to access that information
- it's **not** easy for inappropriate others to access the information.

In office environments, information is increasingly being stored on computers. Such approaches are not yet well developed in services for people with learning disabilities. There are examples of computerised recording systems and it seems likely that, as we all become more computer literate, this will be the norm, rather than the exception. While computers have many advantages it should not be thought that they solve storage and retrieval problems – anyone who has ever tried to find 'that letter I word processed last June' will appreciate this!

Confidentiality and data protection

Confidentiality requires that we '*respect the privacy of service users by taking responsible care of information gained during professional activity, and, in the absence of special circumstances, divulging it only with permission*' (Prince, 2000).

Most of us don't want our personal business talked about in public or displayed on the wall. People with learning disabilities are at much greater risk of breaches of their confidentiality because of living their lives in more 'public' circumstances. Such breaches are only justified where there is evidence that the person might be in danger (eg. of abuse) if the information is not passed on. Concerns about confidentiality should not affect everyday working practices involving the sharing of information. Staff have a duty to work as part of a team and the sharing of information is part of this.

At times, information may be held back from staff on a 'need-to-know' basis, where it is thought that the sharing of the information might harm the person or their reputation significantly. This is often a tricky judgement. Staff should be given information that helps them to do their job in supporting service users but, like us all, are subject to prejudice and bias, and may respond inappropriately to an individual because of some aspect of their history. However, staff should certainly not be denied relevant information if this would put their own or others' safety at risk.

The Data Protection Act (1998) lays out eight principles. All data must be:

1 processed fairly and lawfully
2 obtained and used only for specified and lawful purposes
3 adequate, relevant and not excessive
4 accurate and, where necessary, kept up to date
5 kept for no longer than necessary
6 processed in accordance with the individual's rights
7 kept secure
8 transferred only to countries that offer adequate data protection.

These principles apply both to data recorded electronically and in paper form. Individuals do have a general right of access to information held about them, although information may be withheld if it can be established that it would not be in the person's best interests to see it. The Data Protection Act imposes legal obligations on organisations, which are primarily about following good practice. This tends to lead to a more respectful and objective approach to the recording of information as there is the possibility that the person being written about might request to see this information.

Involving service users

We must always remember that the reason we keep records and handle information in the ways described is to benefit service users. *'Nothing about us without us'* means that we should always consider how the records we are keeping can be made accessible to people with learning disabilities and whether they can be involved in the record-keeping process. There are a number of things to think about here.

- Does the person know that records are being kept? Unless there is a very good reason, they ought to know and be happy about it – imagine finding out, by chance, that someone has been keeping records about your bowel movements without telling you! – and, as far as possible, understand why the records are being kept.
- If the person objects to the records being kept you need to consider

with your colleagues and manager what you should do. There are many circumstances in which you will decide that you need to keep a record anyway (eg. because you have a duty of care to the person), but you should take their objections seriously and consider whether there are alternative, more acceptable ways of doing what you feel you need to do.

- Sometimes it will be more acceptable to the person if they are involved in the record-keeping process, eg. by ticking the boxes on your chart, or by keeping their own record. Service user involvement will be much easier if the recording system is structured and simple to use. As is so often the case, making something accessible to a person with disabilities also makes it more accessible and easier to use for the person without disabilities.

- Service user involvement will be considerably enhanced by presenting things in a 'language' they can understand. In some cases (eg. if the person was brought up speaking Punjabi) this may mean employing a translator. In other cases it may mean ensuring that information is available in Braille, or Makaton symbols, or whatever the individual's preferred mode of communication is. People who can't write or make marks shouldn't be restricted from keeping records – a tape recorder may provide the means of an excellent and accessible record.

Summary

Handling information is a central part of working with people with learning disabilities. Good practice involves:

- being clear about why we need the information
- collecting only the information we need
- making sure that we collect accurate information that can be easily used
- storing information securely but making sure it is accessible to those who need it
- respecting confidentiality
- acting lawfully, in line with the Data Protection Act
- involving service users as much as possible.

Most importantly, good practice involves using the information that has been gathered and stored so that we, ourselves, act in ways that are consistent with the best information about a person's needs and that we are constantly striving to learn (from the records of our own and others' experiences) how to do a better job.

Further reading

Prince K (1996) *Boring Records? Communication, speech and writing in social work*. London: Jessica Kingsley Publishers.

United Kingdom Central Council for Nursing, Midwifery and Health Visiting (1998) *Guidelines for Records and Record Keeping*. London: UKCC.

References

Mansell J, McGill P and Emerson E (2001) Development and evaluation of innovative residential services for people with severe intellectual disability and serious challenging behavior. *International Review of Research in Mental Retardation* **24** 245–298.

Prince K (2000) Confidentiality. In: M Davies (Ed) *The Blackwell Encyclopaedia of Social Work* pp74–75. Oxford: Blackwell.

Chapter 9

Looking through a different lens

Supporting people with autistic spectrum disorders

Key words
social interaction, triad of impairments, communication, sensory processing, structure and routine

For most of us, the first few years of our lives are a period of rapid and intense learning. It is during these first few years and months that we learn to understand our world through our responses and those of our primary caregiver (usually our mother). She smiles and you smile back – a bond is made and maintained.

For people with an autistic spectrum disorder (ASD), some of this learning and development, that most of us take for granted and never even realise is happening, either doesn't happen, only happens in parts, or is significantly delayed. This is why ASD is described as a *lifelong developmental disability*. So Mum smiles, but you don't recognise it as something to respond to. Dad talks to you and you don't have a clue why he is making those funny noises, but he seems to expect something back and you don't understand what. Maybe you hear the musical variance in people's speech, but not the words. Perhaps you hear the words but cannot put them together to make any sense. Your world becomes increasingly filled by people who all want something from you – a response, a smile, an activity – and you cannot understand what they want or why they want it, let alone provide it on demand. You cannot predict or control what these people do or say. So you cope by retreating into your own world and the safety of things you *can* control – your own body, which does what you want it to, when you want it to (most of the time!), videos or DVDs, which run the same story with the same words each time you play them, or a favourite toy that always does the same thing each time. As you get older, you may find that asking the same question gets you a certain reply every time, or that going to the same pub on the same day every week is good. Loud noises may really hurt your ears, some smells might be totally overpowering, and, at times, what you are seeing may not make any sense to you. Donna Williams (1996), an author with an ASD herself, says:

> 'Reality to an autistic person is a confusing, interacting mass of events, people, places, sounds and sights. There seems to be no clear boundaries, order or meaning to anything. A large part of my life is spent just trying to work out the pattern behind everything. Set routines, times, particular routes and rituals all help to get order into an unbearably chaotic life.'

What is an autistic spectrum disorder?

Autism (and the spectrum of autistic disorders) is a lifelong developmental disorder that affects the way the brain processes information, for which there is no cure. People with ASDs therefore perceive, understand and respond to the world in a different way to those without ASD, resulting in difficulties making sense of the world, communicating and relating to others. Autism is an 'invisible' disorder as there are generally no outward physical signs that someone is autistic. This can make it very difficult for other people to understand why someone is behaving in the way they are when they 'look' quite normal.

It is currently thought that approximately two to six people in every 1,000 will have an ASD, with approximately four males to every female. Recent trends suggest that the diagnosis of ASDs is increasing by about 10–17% per year. Estimates of the proportion of people with ASDs who have a learning disability vary considerably, and figures have been quoted from around 25–30% to 65–70%. The National Autistic Society suggests that just below 50% is most likely. In order to receive a diagnosis of ASD, people need to show difficulties in three main areas. These are known as the 'triad of impairments' (see *Box 1*). Wendy Lawson (2001), a writer with autism, points out that this term implies she is *'damaged, ruined, injured or faulty'* in these areas, which is unhelpful, whereas in fact she is simply *'different'* to *'neuro-typicals'* (people without autism).

> ## Box 1: Triad of impairments
> - **Impairment in social interaction** leading to difficulty with peer relationships, non-verbal behaviour, sharing interest with others and taking turns.
> - **Impairment in communication** leading to difficulty with verbal communication, starting or sustaining a conversation, unusual use of words and poor imagination making it difficult to envisage the future.
> - **Impairment in imagination** leading to difficulties predicting consequences of actions, obsessive interests, repetitive stereotyped activities and inflexible routines.

Pattern and range of impairments

Research in the recent past has come up with three main theories to describe some of what is happening, or not happening, in the brains of people with an ASD. None of these theories can account for all the difficulties a person with autism might experience, but they could each account for a part of the picture.

Lack of empathy

Very young children will generally think that other people are thinking the same thing as they are. Research with normally developing children has shown that at around the age of four most children can understand that other people may believe or think something different to what they themselves *believe* or *think* in a certain situation, and that others may have a different view of the world to that of their own. By the age of six, children can generally understand that other people may also *feel* something different to what they feel in a particular situation. This ability to understand that other people are capable of having different beliefs and desires to your own is called having a 'theory of mind'. Researchers have found that children with an ASD often fail the Sally Anne task – a psychological test (see *Box 2*, overleaf). Many researchers have claimed that people with an ASD have difficulty with, or lack completely, a theory of mind (Baron-Cohen, 1995), which might help explain some of their social and communication difficulties. This can lead to a tendency to be very honest about things as they may have difficulty in telling lies, and difficulty empathising with other people's feelings.

> ## Box 2: The Sally Anne task (Frith, 1989)
> This is Sally. Sally has a basket. This is Anne. Anne has a box. Sally has a marble. She puts the marble into her basket. Sally goes out for a walk. Anne takes the marble out of the basket, and puts it into the box. Now Sally comes back. She wants to play with her marble. Where will Sally look for her marble?

Taking in information

People with an ASD have also been shown to have difficulty 'seeing the wood for the trees'. They may be extremely good at seeing the detail in a picture or a problem, but are unable or find it difficult to fit the pieces of the information together to form an overall picture or whole. This has been suggested (first by Frith, 1989) to be a result of having *weak central coherence* and is a description of the way in which their brain processes information. It might also explain some of the special talents and peaks in performance that people with autism might experience, such as being particularly good at tasks or jobs requiring an eye for detail. Several authors with an ASD have described themselves as only being able to process incoming information on one 'channel' at a time. This may mean they cannot listen and look at something at the same time, and may lose concentration halfway through a sentence – only taking in a part of it.

Mental flexibility

Executive function refers to the ability to plan and organise, sustain attention, control impulses, initiate actions and exercise mental flexibility among other things. It has been suggested that people with an ASD have difficulty with *executive dysfunction* (Ozonoff *et al*, 1991), which can result in difficulty with planning, consequences, perseverative behaviours, rigid thinking and problems with inhibiting responses to situations. This might explain the stereotyped behaviours and narrow interests that many people with autism experience. The research evidence, however, remains mixed about the extent of these difficulties and whether they are exclusive to people with autism.

The spectrum of autism

Classic autism was first recognised in the 1940s by American psychiatrist Leo Kanner, who described the symptoms and behaviours among a group of learning disabled children. Shortly after, Hans Asperger described similar symptoms and behaviours among a much more able group of children with superior language skills (Asperger's syndrome). In the late 1970s Lorna Wing proposed the idea of an autistic *spectrum*, which better describes the full range of children with varying intellectual levels and patterns of social, communication and imagination difficulties. Today, ASDs are thought to affect 90 in 10,000 people (0.9% of the population).

Autism is one of five disorders described under the umbrella term of pervasive developmental disorders. The others include Asperger's syndrome, Rett syndrome, childhood disintegrative disorder and pervasive developmental disorder, not otherwise specified (PDD-NOS). All five are considered to be life-long conditions linked to a delay or significant problem in early development resulting in social, communication and behavioural difficulties.

What effect do these 'impairments' have?

The ability to communicate and interact with others around us is central to the way we experience, the way we fit in with, and the way we function in our world. Difficulties with these key aspects of life can result in people with autism finding unusual and different ways of understanding, coping and behaving in relation to the world around them.

Communication difficulties

People with autism have usually had difficulties with early language development. Often they do not learn to speak until much later than their peers, may develop limited or very unusual speech patterns or have no verbal language at all. Sometimes children will appear to have normal early language development and can then lose their language skills at around age two (this is now known as childhood disintegrative disorder). They may use peculiar words and sounds that only have meaning to them, or their language might consist largely of learnt phrases and words copied from elsewhere, which they use out of context. Some people repeat back what is said to them, either immediately or after a delay (echolalia). Pronoun reversal is also common – referring to themselves as 'he' or 'hers' or by name rather than 'I', 'my' or 'me'.

People with Asperger's syndrome may talk excessively, in a flat monotone, about things they are particularly interested in. Their conversation might be very one-sided with little or no turn-taking, and might be faster or slower than is 'normal'.

Communication in its broadest sense can be very difficult for someone with an ASD to understand and use. If someone does not understand why people would want to talk to each other, or spend time interacting, they can become scared or anxious about approaching others and communicating with them. They may assume that they know what others want and think (theory of mind difficulties) and therefore not see the point of communicating a particular wish or need. Difficulties with communication can therefore lead to high levels of frustration and anxiety and, in the absence of any alternative method, may be expressed through challenging behaviour.

Social interaction

Relationships and interactions with other people are often a minefield for people with autism. The subtle rules of interaction, which most of us pick up as we grow up, are a necessary part of living and getting on with others. People with autism may need to be taught the appropriate amount of personal space to maintain when near other people, how to take turns in conversation, what might be seen as rude, what constitutes a friendship, how to co-operate in a group situation and how to recognise, and react to, different emotions in themselves and others. They may desperately want relationships with others – to have friends like everyone around them – but be unable to develop or sustain such relationships.

Typically, non-verbal communication, such as gestures, facial expressions, body language and eye contact are also lacking or diminished in children and adults with an ASD.

Difficulties with imagination, perception and thought processes

Most of us use our imaginations to help us predict what might happen in a particular situation, what the consequences of a certain behaviour might be, whether someone will be pleased or unhappy with us or what we would like to see happen in our lives. However, people who find it difficult to imagine situations in advance, or more abstract concepts like feelings, can find life very difficult.

People with autism often perceive the world in a very different way to other people because when they absorb information their brain may process it in different ways. Someone with autism may not be able to listen, walk and visually take in his/her surroundings all at the same time. Their brains may favour one channel, so while they might listen to you, they may have no idea how they have arrived at a different place. Or, while they watch, they may not be able to monitor the volume of their speech, or may even lose track of the words they are using. When new experiences happen, someone with autism may not be able to access information about past experiences, which will tell them how to respond. The connections the brain automatically makes, which help us to take in information in a variety of ways, carry out actions and respond to others, may take much longer to happen for someone with autism – or they may not happen at all.

What can the research tell us about causes of autism?

There is good evidence to suggest that autism is caused by a range of factors that affect brain development. Research has shown a strong link with genetic factors, with the view that several genes probably interact to cause a susceptibility to the disorder. Interaction between the environment and the genes may then play a major role in triggering the disorder.

Supporting people with autistic spectrum disorders

While some may feel that there is little to be gained by a diagnosis of ASD in adulthood, it does help us to begin to understand how best to support someone with this pattern of differences. Even though there is no cure for autism, structured support and the management of a person's environment can make a big difference to the life of someone with autism. Every person with autism is as individual and different from each other in the same way that every person without autism is. However, there are several areas of difficulty common to most people with autism, and these serve as a good starting point for understanding how best to support someone with an ASD. Anxiety plays a huge role in influencing the way someone with autism responds or behaves and therefore many of the following suggestions aim to reduce levels of anxiety.

Structure, routine and predictability

When your world is chaotic, unpredictable and therefore quite frightening, the need for structure, routine and predictability becomes greater, and can help to reduce anxiety a lot. Some people with autism benefit from a clear structure to their day and week, to help them predict what is about to happen next. Picture timetables can be made using photographs or symbols to show what activities are taking place today, punctuated by meal and break times (breakfast, activity, coffee break, activity, lunch, activity, tea break, activity etc). For many people who have difficulty with the concept of time, meals and breaks are recognisable points by which the passing of time can be marked. Some people will like to have a whole week's activities planned out, others will only be able to manage a day at a time. Even this may provoke too much anxiety in some, who will manage better just knowing what the next activity is, and no more.

The support worker role

The general principles of supporting someone with a learning disability may not always be as straightforward when supporting someone with autism. A basic understanding of the way autism affects people is necessary to start with. Extra training for staff teams on ASDs might be a good way of achieving this. Sometimes you may find you are advocating for particular ways of doing things with the person, and having to explain to others why they need it to be that way. Offering choice is a good example of this – individuals with autism often find it very difficult and anxiety-provoking to be offered a range of things to choose from – and can find it easier simply to be offered a choice of only two things at a time.

Accommodation and flexibility are key – often it is easier to change the environment or activity rather than try and change the person's behaviour. The support worker can anticipate and help prepare the person for change and can recognise in advance situations that are likely to cause them anxiety or distress, while maintaining very clear boundaries (which will help them feel safe). Clear, concrete explanations of difficult situations help someone with autism to understand. Drafting clear 'rules' for situations, or 'contracts' clearly stating what both parties expect in a situation is helpful. Repeatedly practising difficult social situations with role play can also help someone learn how to respond appropriately.

Change is another thing that is often difficult, whether it is temporary or permanent change. Some people may need advance warning of any impending changes to help them adapt to the idea and be reassured about it, while others will find that too much notice increases their anxiety. The optimum time can be worked out for each individual. It may take someone with an ASD much longer to adapt to a move to a new college or living arrangement, and transitions should be planned carefully with several 'acclimatisation' visits to help the person adapt. For many people living in supported accommodation, regular changes in support staff can be a major issue. When a keyworker leaves and a new staff member, or unknown agency employee, appears it can result in a big change in behaviour. Several staff changes over a short period of time can be disastrous for the person with an ASD.

Endings can also be difficult as they represent a change of activity. There are several ways to help someone move from one activity to another, such as using an 'endings box' into which the objects being used are placed.

A kitchen timer can be set to warn the person at intervals that the end is approaching. This has the advantage of being an inanimate object, and is less likely to provoke an angry response. Cue cards (ie. photos of the next activity, destination etc) have also been used successfully to help people move on.

Increasing visual, and reducing verbal, support can make a big difference if you can try to 'put yourself inside the head' of the person with autism, and imagine the world as they see it. This can help you to understand why the person reacts in the way they do, how to motivate them, and most importantly help to build a relationship. Many early intervention programmes for children with autism work on supporting the adult to enter the child's psychological space and engage with them at their level. Try joining in with someone's favourite activity, enjoying what they are doing and after time perhaps extending it a little to see if they will follow. In this way trust can be built up. Trust is often a vital ingredient in supporting someone with an ASD. The world itself appears unpredictable and untrustworthy, so they need to be able to trust that you are not going to put them in situations they find difficult to bear. A part of this is being able to maintain clear boundaries for someone who cannot put any boundaries in place for themselves. It may also involve anticipating and translating the world for them. Maintaining a positive view and positive personal energy is always beneficial.

Specific therapies/techniques

There are several therapies and techniques that have proved to be successful when working with someone with an ASD.

TEACCH (Treatment and Education of Autistic and related Communication-handicapped Children)

This approach is person-centred and focuses on the person with autism and the development of a programme around this person's skills, interests and needs, rather than trying to get that person to fit a non-autistic model of behaviour. Individual strengths and interests are cultivated and it is recognised that relative strengths in some areas (visual, memory, an eye for detail) can become the basis for successful adult functioning. Making use of these interests also increases motivation and understanding. On a practical level, the approach is known for its emphasis on promoting a calm, low-stress environment with clutter-free, distraction-free rooms (white walls with no pictures) to help focus and reduce sensory overload. Visual information, such as daily timetables using photos of activities and mealtimes can help greatly.

Social stories and comic strip conversations

There are several books available on the use of social stories with people with autism. This method originated in Canada with Carol Gray, who has developed a specific format for compiling short stories that aim to teach someone a social skill they have not previously learnt or understood for whatever reason. They describe the 'problem' situation/behaviour in a few clear sentences, then aim to describe other people's perspective on it and end with a directive sentence guiding the person towards the alternative response/behaviour.

Comic strip conversations also originate from Carol Gray (1994), and provide a visual way of communicating in a non-threatening, anxiety-reducing way with someone who finds the social aspects of communication difficult and might struggle to comprehend the quick exchange of information that happens in a normal spoken conversation. By drawing cartoon pictures of a situation, thought bubbles, speech bubbles and using colours for different emotions, people with autism can be helped to explain or discuss situations they would otherwise find difficult.

Case study: John

John is a young man with a learning disability and autism. He has always had particular difficulties with understanding the need to bath and change his clothes regularly. He usually sleeps in his clothes and will only wear one particular set of clothes. No amount of explaining and reminding from support staff has been able to get John to change his behaviour.

A social story was put together, describing to John why people need to bath or shower and change their clothes, giving other people's perspective on how they felt if he did not wash or change and ending with a directive sentence saying he would try to wash and change his clothes. It also directed him to the bathroom where another social story 'talked' him through bathing step by step, describing and explaining what needed to be done, and finished with a sentence guiding him to put on his pyjamas. A duplicate set of clothing was bought and John was supported by staff to choose a set of new pyjamas, which he took to the bathroom with him to put on after his bath.

A very simple solution – but it worked! By removing the interpersonal aspect and giving John a clear, concrete set of explanations and instructions to follow, he was able to wash and change his clothes on a daily basis.

Intensive interaction

See *Chapter 12* on people with profound and multiple learning disabilities.

Auditory and sensory integration therapy

Many people with an ASD are hypersensitive to sounds. Loud noises, babies crying or particular noises may be unbearable for them (sometimes giving physical pain), causing them to put their hands over their ears, become highly anxious or agitated. Some cope by blocking out the noise, appearing deaf and retreating into their own world. A 'sensory audit' of a person's environment can often show many potential causes of sensory overload and anxiety. Auditory integration training is a method of desensitising the hearing mechanism so that intrusive sounds can be ignored. In this way, it is claimed that noisy environments become tolerable, and people are better able to communicate, concentrate and cope.

Sensory integration therapy aims to help people be able to use several of their senses at the same time ie. to use their sight, hearing, smell, taste and touch, in an integrated way rather than only being able to process on one channel at a time.

Social skills training

Most of us learn from an early age the rules of social interaction and society – what is acceptable and unacceptable behaviour, how to meet and greet, what is polite and rude and how to be with other people. We learn much of this without any direct teaching but by observing and copying others, by generalising from comments made by our parents, and from the desire to 'fit in' with our peers. However, for people on the autistic spectrum this social learning does not seem to happen and they can find it very difficult to manage the subtleties of interpersonal behaviour that we so take for granted. Social skills training can be run in small group settings or carried out individually (if a group is too anxiety provoking for someone) to help people learn, by rote, the acceptable way to react and respond in particular situations. These groups have been shown to be very helpful for people on the autistic spectrum, while promoting greater confidence, self-esteem and positive interactions with others.

Anxiety management

High levels of anxiety are a very common, sometimes overwhelming problem for many people with an ASD. It can affect people in different ways – some may turn inward, spending more and more time alone in their room as they are the only person they can depend on to be predictable and understandable. Others may try to take more and more control of their world to make it predictable – insisting you give a particular response to a particular question over and over. There are many steps that can be taken to help prevent anxiety from building up and to help calm someone once they begin to become anxious or agitated. Most relaxation and meditation techniques have repetition at heart, which is usually liked by people with ASDs (see *Box 3*).

Box 3: Possible relaxation strategies
- Build in a relaxing routine the person is known to enjoy at particularly stressful points in the day (eg. on return from day services)
- Model and teach deep-breathing exercises
- Teach a mantra to say over and over with them when stressed ('I'm OK', 'It's all going to be OK', 'Stay calm')
- Regular physical exercise sessions
- Ensure there is a 'low stress' room the person can withdraw to when becoming overloaded, somewhere preferably with pale coloured walls, few distractions and possibly some calming lighting
- Offer calming music to listen to or some favourite music they like
- If being with others is too difficult or arousing, alternate activities and mealtimes with periods alone to calm down

Diet therapy
There is some research following the idea that autism is the result of a metabolic disorder where the gut's immune function is impaired. In order to combat this, many people with autism have benefited from following a gluten (wheat and some other cereal products) and casein (milk and dairy produce) free diet. This has been shown to lead to a reduction in 'autistic behaviours' in some people, but does not work for everyone. Vitamin and mineral deficiencies are also found due to the leaky gut problem, and some people have found a regime of vitamin and mineral supplements to be helpful.

Medication
There is very little evidence for the effectiveness of drugs in helping to reduce autistic behaviours, and no single medication has been found to be helpful for everyone with an ASD. Despite that, drugs are still prescribed by many psychiatrists to help control the behaviour of people with a learning disability and an ASD. Those drugs that are prescribed are usually known to be

effective with different conditions (such as depression, schizophrenia or epilepsy), and have been tried out with autism to see if they have any effect.

The drugs most commonly prescribed to learning disabled clients with autism are anti-depressants to help calm and reduce depression, atypical anti-psychotics to help reduce aggression and anti-epileptics to stabilise mood. Tranquillisers are also sometimes prescribed for use in single doses – only in cases of extreme agitation.

There is some debate about the correct dosages of these potentially highly toxic drugs to be used. Results of research into dosages with this patient group have been disappointing. Dr Temple Grandin has suggested that people with an ASD are very sensitive to medication and therefore only require a minute dosage (Grandin, 1998).

Interpreting behaviour

It is important to remember that while everyone with autism shares the difficulty of making sense of the world, they differ in how that difficulty might manifest itself. For some, life can become very caught up in various obsessions (preoccupations with parts of objects, a particular subject such as dinosaurs, certain TV programmes), repetitive behaviours (hand-flapping, rocking, spinning, head-banging, asking particular questions) and routines (having to complete a set bedtime routine, or mealtime routine every day). For many, being interrupted during one of these compulsive rituals can lead to great distress and agitation. Often repetitive, stereotypical behaviours serve as a way to de-stress and calm, by blocking out anxiety-provoking irritants, or they can provide stimulation. In an unpredictable world, a predictable routine can provide a degree of certainty and a feeling of safety.

Emotions are complex, abstract and difficult to understand for most people – even those without a developmental delay. People with an ASD frequently have great difficulty with emotions and may have trouble understanding what others are feeling and also what they are feeling themselves. This can lead to people expressing their emotions in unexpected or harmful ways. If you do not recognise, and cannot name, anger or sadness it can be very overwhelming and frightening to be overtaken by such an emotion. By learning to name the concrete bodily reactions that accompany each emotion, people with autism can be helped to recognise and, in time, attain a degree of control over their emotions.

As well as poor emotional feedback, people with an ASD often have trouble identifying physical and sensory feedback. This may result in difficulty recognising feelings such as pain or hunger. Someone may not be able to tell you, and indeed may not be able to identify for themselves, if they are hurting somewhere. Instead, they may communicate this distress by self-harming, becoming agitated or distressed or by withdrawing. Alternatively, they may not communicate the problem at all. Physical symptoms can be misinterpreted as a result. It is therefore advisable to rule out a physical cause for any change in behaviour if someone is unable to communicate such feelings.

Effective communication

People with an ASD can have difficulties with communication in different ways to people who have a learning disability but not autism. There are several things we can do to help try and make what we are saying easier to process for someone with autism.

- Use concrete speech – be very clear, literal and positive in what you are saying (ie. 'do this', instead of 'don't do that'). Avoid abstract and metaphorical speech, similes and over-elaboration.
- Reduce the amount of words you use to explain something – simplify, slow down and repeat.
- If the message is important, reduce any external distractions first (such as noise, other people etc) to help processing of the information.
- Be consistent – use exactly the same words for instructions every time – that way you are predictable and safe.
- Use someone's particular passionate interests to engage with them.
- Avoid emotional language, such as too much praise or talk about feelings.
- Some people with autism do not use the words 'me' and 'I', and confuse them with 'he' and 'she', or might refer to themselves by name. If this is the case, try not to use those words yourself – call them by name too.
- Consider writing, typing or drawing side by side to communicate with someone, taking the interpersonal contact part of communication away.
- Some people with autism can find touch unpleasant. If you need to touch someone, ask them if it is OK first or overtly signal what you intend doing and give them time to adjust.

For further ideas see *Chapter 6* on communication.

Further information and support

There are many very helpful organisations and resources available on ASDs. The National Autistic Society (www.nas.org.uk) provides a wealth of information and links to local and national services, research bodies and parent/carer support networks, as well as organising training and conferences around the country for carers and support staff. Locally, members of your nearest learning disability community team will have experience of working with people with ASDs and should be able to offer advice and support. There is also a rapidly expanding range of books being published by people with autism writing about their own experiences, understandings and difficulties. These provide an excellent introduction to understanding the very different way a person with autism experiences the world.

Perhaps the most important thing any of us can do to try and help someone with an ASD is to try and understand what it is like for them – trying to 'get inside their head' and see out through their eyes can give an invaluable insight into that person's fears, responses, behaviours and feelings, and how to help them. From that starting point a trusting relationship can be built.

Further reading

Attwood T (1998) *Asperger Syndrome: A guide for parents and professionals*. London: Jessica Kingsley Publishers.
  The Asperger bible!

Baron-Cohen S (1993) *Autism: The facts*. Oxford: Oxford Paperbacks.
  The basic facts of autism – a good first reader.

Caldwell P (2005) *Learning the Language*. Brighton: Pavilion Publishing (Brighton) Ltd.
  Video demonstrating the use of Intensive Interaction with a young man with autism.

Clements J (2005) *People with Autism Behaving Badly*. London: Jessica Kingsley Publishers.
  Hands-on book detailing strategies to help resolve common problem behaviours. The book is organised around the common messages conveyed by behaviours and some of the underlying issues that drive these messages.

Howley M and Arnold E (2005) *Revealing the Hidden Social Code: Social stories for people with ASD*. London: Jessica Kingsley Publishers.

Lawson W (2001) *Understanding and Working with the Spectrum of Autism*. London: Jessica Kingsley Publishers.
  An author with an ASD discusses ways to address problems such as anxiety, obsessive behaviours, social understanding and communication from an insider viewpoint.

Williams D (2005) *Blah, Blah, Blah* (DVD). Available from:
www.donnawilliams.net/blahdvd.0.html
> Lecture by author with ASD on communication. Gives invaluable insight into understanding effects of autism.

Wing L (2002) *The Autistic Spectrum: A guide for parents and professionals*. London: Constable and Robinson.
> Basic introduction to the field of autistic spectrum disorders covering development and way of helping children and adults with autism. Written by professional in the field who is also a parent of a person with an ASD.

References

Baron-Cohen S (1995) *Mindblindness: An essay on autism and theory of mind*. Cambridge, Massachusetts: MIT Press/Bradford Books.

Frith U (1989) *Autism: Explaining the enigma*. Oxford: Basil Blackwell.

Grandin T (1998) *Evaluating the Effects of Medication*. Paper available online at:
www.autism.org/temple/meds.html.

Gray C (1994) *Comic Strip Conversations*. Arlington, Texas: Future Horizons.

Lawson W (2001) *Understanding and Working with the Spectrum of Autism*. London: Jessica Kingsley Publishers.

Ozonoff S, Pennington B and Rogers S (1991) Executive function deficits in high functioning autistic children: relationship to theory of mind. *Journal of Child Psychology and Psychiatry* **32** (7) 1081–1106.

Williams D (1996) *Autism – An inside-out approach*. London: Jessica Kingsley Publishers.

Marian Marsham
Lisa Poynor

Chapter 10

Better help, better health

Enabling and supporting people with learning disabilities to access healthcare

Key words

accessing care, assessment, communication, recognising health needs, physical vulnerability

People with learning disabilities face a triple challenge when accessing healthcare. Research suggests they frequently have greater than average health needs (see *Box 1*), yet use health services disproportionately less than the general population. When they do use health services they are more likely to experience a dissatisfying service resulting in poorer health outcomes.

Box 1: Conditions that occur more commonly in learning disabled population

- Epilepsy
- Sensory impairment
- Mobility problems
- Gastrointestinal problems
- Feeding and nutritional problems
- Obesity
- Respiratory disease
- Mental health problems
- Hormone imbalance

For people whose learning disability has a genetic cause there may be other particular health problems that relate to the cause of their learning disability, such as Down's syndrome and hypothyroid, Prader-Willi syndrome and obesity, or tuberous sclerosis and epilepsy.

People with learning disabilities may experience health inequality caused by wider determinants of health, such as poverty, social deprivation and lifestyle choices. This is in addition to the barriers relating to their disability, which can include the way services are organised and designed, the discriminatory attitudes of healthcare workers, miscommunication and lack of information in easy-to-understand formats.

The impact of these barriers and inequalities can often be that treatable illnesses remain undetected until they've reached a stage where treatment is less effective and the negative experience of illness is greater. For some this can mean suffering unnecessarily, or even dying at an earlier age than their non-disabled peers. Therefore, special steps need to be taken to ensure that everyone can have an equal chance to enjoy the best health possible.

These issues are recognised in the white paper, Valuing People, which recommends specific strategies for services to adopt to improve the health of people with learning disabilities, such as health action plans (HAPs), the training of health facilitators and regular health checks.

A HAP is a person-centred document outlining what the person and those supporting them need to do to promote optimum health. The Department of Health suggests that a good HAP includes information from a health check.

The title Health Facilitator can really be applied to anyone who takes the lead in supporting the person to access healthcare and have his/her health needs understood and met.

Recognising health need

'From my point of view the health checks make the patient and the family feel less outside of the service – less taboo.' (Jo, Practice Nurse)

Generally, health services in the UK are reliant on the person identifying a problem and initiating contact with their GP. This is the first step for recognising and meeting health need. However, for people with learning disabilities it can be different. For example:

- they may not recognise symptoms of ill-health
- they may not be able to explain symptoms to someone who could help
- they (or the person who is helping them) may not appreciate the significance of the symptoms.

Uptake rates for screening programmes and routine check ups for people with learning disabilities are low. Health checks are a good way of ensuring that health needs are recognised and HAPs can help to ensure that needs are met.

John's story

John is a middle-aged man with severe learning disability. He was seen for a health check and his practice nurse commented on his fatigue – the staff supporting him reported that John had developed a habit of waking up at night to go to the toilet, which wasn't a problem as they had night staff. The practice nurse made a referral to the continence service and John's enlarged prostate was diagnosed.

Recognising health needs: top tips for positive practice

- Get to know the person you support and think about your role in promoting healthy lifestyle choices.
- Get to know what is usual for them so you can recognise when anything changes.
- Spend regular time talking to them about their health to find out if anything has changed and to gauge their understanding of their own needs and health generally.
- Use a health check tool to ensure that you cover everything in the first instance.
- Use accessible material to aid communication and understanding.
- Support the person to obtain health checks and take advantage of national screening programmes.
- If you have any doubts or concerns about a person's health, always seek advice about what to do next from an appropriate source, such as a GP, pharmacist, NHS Direct, community nurse or your manager.
- If you work with groups of people with learning disabilities, consider spending time on health promotion issues such as healthy lifestyles and healthy choices.

Anne's story

Anne, who has moderate learning disability and anxiety disorder, told her sister that she had fallen over and hurt her leg. Her sister arranged for Anne's GP to visit and was there with Anne when he came. There was no visible wound so they assumed that Anne was exaggerating and being over anxious, and did not advise any investigations. Her support worker visited later the same day and felt that, although it was possible that Anne could be exaggerating her symptoms, it warranted proper investigation. She called an ambulance and accompanied Anne to hospital where she was treated for a fractured leg.

Seeking and accessing care

'I'm glad my support worker comes to appointments with me. I get muddled, the doctor is nice but she talks quickly. She asks me if I have understood but I don't like to say if I haven't.' (Fay, service user)

The white paper, Valuing People set a number of targets, including – all people with learning disabilities were to be registered with a GP by June 2004, to have a health facilitator identified by spring 2003 and to have a HAP by June 2005.

People with learning disabilities may need support accessing primary care, which involves a number of skills, such as using a telephone, telling the time, articulating needs to a stranger, planning, organising transport, preparation and anxiety management.

Accessibility is not just about physical access like ramps, but also about understanding the consultation, treatment and following advice given.

Janet's story

Janet's support worker noticed she kept rubbing her eyes so she made a GP appointment for her. Janet kept the appointment, and nothing further was said about the matter within the supported living home where Janet lived. A few days later when Janet returned from a stay with her mother, the support worker found a note from Janet's mother saying all was ok with the eye drops. This surprised the support worker, as they were unaware that eye drops had been prescribed, what they were for or how long Janet should use them. When they asked Janet what the GP had said, she couldn't remember. Janet would have been glad to have support at the appointment, which was clearly needed, had it been offered.

Seeking and accessing care: top tips for positive practice

- Ensure the person you support is registered with a GP and that the GP knows they have a learning disability. You can contact your local Patient Advice and Liaison Services (PALS) for assistance with registering.
- If required, negotiate optimum appointment times, such as the first or double appointments.
- Enable the person you support to prepare by helping them understand what their appointment is for, what might happen at the appointment and what the possible outcomes might be.
- Give timely reminders about appointments by phone or text.

- Give opportunities to ask questions and explore what support is needed.
- It is essential for any supporter accompanying the person to be well acquainted with them and their current status so that an accurate and full picture can be conveyed to the doctor.
- During the appointment facilitate effective communication between the person and the doctor – don't be afraid to ask questions if there is anything you yourself don't understand or if you think something has been missed. Don't be afraid to challenge politely if you feel the person's needs are not being fully appreciated for any reason. In certain circumstances the consultation may not be the best arena for challenge, and you may also wish to seek support with this eg. from your line manager, PALS or community team for people with learning disabilities (CTPLD).
- Write things down – prepare questions for the doctor in advance. Anticipate the information you may need to give to the doctor. During the consultation write down any advice given so you can be clear about this when feeding back or reviewing the consultation with the person.
- After the appointment debrief the main points together – try to gauge understanding and views – and look at what you might need to work on together before any follow-up appointments.
- Consider what help the person you support needs in order to carry out the advice given effectively, for example, if they were prescribed medication do they know how to take it and tell if it is working?

Diagnosis treatment and support

'Lizzie was in hospital and I visited her regularly. I had a number of concerns (no help choosing meals, leg ulcers not dressed, legs not elevated, no bath offered and a mix up with her medication), which I continually brought up with staff, with little sustained improvement. I went to the community nurse after a few days as I knew the ward team would not be able to ignore her – I was right, things improved for Lizzie instantly.' (Vicki, Support Worker)

The doctor/clinician will need to hear the fullest possible account of the person's health difficulties, and past events relating to it, to get a realistic picture and arrive at an accurate diagnosis, if one is possible.

Ill-health is diagnosed by understanding symptoms reported by the patient as well as investigations and tests. This enables the doctor to carry out the most appropriate intervention and prescribe the best treatment for the person. The person may need help to understand exactly what is wrong and what the treatment is. Sometimes their symptoms are interpreted as an integral part of their disability, which can lead to misdiagnosis or to leaving detectable illness untreated – this is called diagnostic overshadowing.

For a treatment or investigation to be given the doctor must seek the patient's informed consent. People with learning disabilities may need help to understand the proposed intervention and consequences of their decision to refuse or accept treatment. They may not have capacity to give consent at all, so the doctor must then act in the person's 'best interests' in consultation with significant others. This can be a very complex process, particularly when capacity or best interests are disputed, and in itself can be a barrier to healthcare. Guidance is given in the Mental Capacity Act (see *Chapter 2*).

People with learning disabilities who require hospital treatment are particularly vulnerable, due to:

- communication difficulties
- diagnostic overshadowing
- additional conditions associated with learning disability not being recognised
- not being able to understand their treatment or illness
- confusion about consent/capacity.

Josh's story

Josh has severe learning disabilities and does not use words to communicate. He had to go hospital for hernia repair surgery. He was visited by his support worker who found him trying to eat his soup with a fork. The support worker also noticed he winced as he moved and was told by the nurse that he had not been given any painkillers because he had not said he was in pain when asked. Once the support worker explained her observations and Josh's needs to the nurses, they administered some pain relief and ensured a healthcare assistant was present when meals were served.

Diagnosis, treatment and support: top tips for positive practice

- Once a diagnosis has been made, find out all you can about the condition so you can advocate and support effectively.
- Allow time to explain the diagnosis, procedures and possible outcomes – try to gauge the person's opinions/capacity with a view to potential consent issues.
- Explore opportunities to increase understanding and reduce anxiety

by using appropriate/accessible materials, arranging visits to the treatment area and practising skills that may be needed during treatment, such as sitting still. You could use role play to rehearse.

- You may wish to enlist specialist support, such as a psychologist or community nurse if there are specific issues, such as anxiety management, needle phobia etc.
- If the treatment involves hospitalisation, communicate with the ward staff at every stage including pre-admission and discharge planning.
- Be aware of any changing health needs – the person you support may be more dependent when ill than when well and may have increased dependency when they are discharged.
- Hospital staff may need help to understand learning disability issues.
- Send in written information about the person and their usual support needs and be prepared to give some information more than once.
- Ask – never assume!

Jo's story

Jo was due to go into hospital for a hip replacement. Her community nurse and key worker helped her complete a 'patient information sheet' for the ward staff about her communication needs, likes and dislikes etc and she also took in her daily care plan, HAP, and a photo of herself with friends to encourage the staff to see her as a whole and valued person. During her stay the home staff made daily contact by phone or visits so they could arrange to be there to support Jo and her treatment team at key times such as her first physiotherapy session and discharge meeting. This helped Jo's hospital stay to be a positive experience for all.

Summary

Accessing healthcare is a process and the person you support may need help at any or all of the respective stages. However, the process does not end once treatment is gained. Healthcare services are now paying more attention to what patients have to say about how services are designed and run in the future. There is a risk that services may develop according to the needs of the most articulate majority. In order to reduce the risk of further inequality, it is just as important to enable people with learning disabilities to participate in patient improvement programmes, individual feedback, consultations, learning disability partnership boards and charities/campaigns, as it is to enable access to healthcare on an individual basis.

Useful resources

There are numerous examples of useful resources developed specifically for people with learning disabilities. Contact your local health promotion service, CTPLD, GP/health centre, local/national charities and campaign groups for advice and accessible materials.

The Mental Capacity Act (2005): www.dca.gov.uk/legal-policy/mental-capacity/index.htm

Find out more about the other white papers: www.dh.gov.uk

Further reading

Dahlgren and Whitehead (1991) *Policies and Strategies to Promote Social Equality in Health.* Stockholm: Institute for Future Studies.

Department of Health (1995) *The Health of the Nation – A strategy for people with learning disabilities.* Oldham: HMSO.

Department of Health (1998) *Signposts for Success in Commissioning and Providing Health Services for People with Learning Disabilities.* London: Department of Health.

Department of Health (1999) *Once a Day.* London: Department of Health.

Department of Health (2001) *Valuing People – A new strategy for learning disability for the 21st Century.* London: Department of Health.

Department of Health (2006) *Our Health, Our Care, Our Say: A new direction for community services.* London: Department of Health.

Disability Rights Commission (2006) *Equal Treatment: Closing the gap – a formal investigation into physical health inequalities experienced by people with learning disability and/or mental health problems.* Stratford upon Avon: DRC.

Kerr M (1998) Primary health care and health gain for people with a learning disability. *Tizard Learning Disability Review* **3** (4) 6–14

Kerr M, Frazer W and Felce D (1996) Primary healthcare for people with a learning disability. *British Journal of Learning Disabilities* **24** (1) 2–8.

Mencap (1997) *Prescription for Change.* London: Mencap.

Mencap (2004) *Treat Me Right!* London: Mencap.

Mencap (2007) *Death by Indifference.* London: Mencap.

Martin DM, Ray A and Wells MB (1997) Health gain through health checks: improving access to primary health care for people with learning disabilities. *Journal of Intellectual Disability Research* **41** (5) 401–408

National Patient Safety Agency (2004) *Understanding the Patient Safety Issues for People with Learning Disability.* London: NPSA.

Turner S and Moss S (1996) The health needs of adults with learning disabilities and the health of the nation strategy. *Journal of Intellectual Disability Research* **40** (5) 438–450.

Chapter 11

Confrontation or communication?

Supporting people whose behaviour challenges us

Key words
internal factors, external factors, antecedent behaviour consequences (ABC), communication, positive prevention strategies, demand avoidance, attention, tangible reinforcement, self-stimulation

What is 'challenging behaviour'?

Those involved in the care of people with learning disabilities are very likely to come across individuals who behave in ways that could be seen as challenging. Some researchers have suggested that approximately 10–15% of people with learning disabilities exhibit challenging behaviour. However, the term 'challenging behaviour' may seem rather vague in that it may cover a very wide range of behaviours. However, there is broad agreement that the term refers to **behaviours that have a negative impact on the person's quality of life or the quality of life of the people with whom they live**.

Two examples will serve to illustrate this range. The first is a man who will sing nursery rhymes at the top of his voice for hours at a time, the second, a man who will attack those around him by biting and scratching. Both behaviours, although very different, have a significant impact for those individuals and those who provide their care. The first person's behaviour would draw attention to the individual in public and irritate carers; the second would provoke fear and anxiety in carers making them reluctant to come into contact with the person. Both of these people would suffer in terms of their quality of life. The 'challenge' would be for carers to reduce the behaviour and, perhaps more importantly, make sure the person enjoyed a better quality of life.

Why do people exhibit challenging behaviour?

When working with people who present challenging behaviour it is inevitable that we will ask ourselves *why* the person does it. This is an extremely important question, as the conclusion will determine what we do to manage the behaviour. For an understanding to be useful, it should give us an indication of what we could do to reduce the behaviour, and also give us some idea of when the behaviour is likely to occur.

Often, the explanations given by carers for challenging behaviour will be things like frustration, anger, spite, greed, sadness, etc. These are all factors that lie within the person, ie. *internal* factors. While they may contain some grains of truth, they are not really useful in the sense described above. They do not give us any ideas about what should be done to prevent or reduce the behaviour; neither do they give us any indication as to when, or under what circumstances, the behaviour is likely to occur. The latter is important information, especially if the behaviour is aggression directed toward carers. If I might get hurt, personally I want to know when the behaviour is likely to happen, so I can be prepared. Therefore, it is generally considered more useful if external explanations are used that involve an understanding of what sort of situations trigger the behaviours. For example, is the behaviour more likely to occur if a request is made of the person, they see something they want but can't get, they are left with nothing to do, or if they are not being given any attention?

Psychologists have developed the antecedent behaviour consequences (ABC) approach to understanding challenging behaviour. This involves identifying the antecedents, or triggers, to the behaviour and also describing what happens as a result of the behaviour – the consequences.

A typical scenario might be:

Antecedent – asked to do the washing up
Behaviour – self-injury and screaming
Consequences – request withdrawn.

In this case, the reason the behaviour occurred was to escape from the demand. Thus, the behaviour can be seen as a form of communication, and the aim of understanding is to attempt to identify what the person is trying to say. Four main communication messages or reasons why people with learning disabilities present challenging behaviour have been identified:

- demand avoidance
- tangible reinforcement
- self-stimulation
- attention.

> **Demand avoidance** would be similar to the above scenario, whereby the individual is rewarded by the removal of a demand.
>
> **Tangible reinforcement** refers to situations where the individual would obtain objects or activities they like as a result of the behaviour.
>
> **Self-stimulation** would be occasions where the behaviour itself is stimulating (and perhaps enjoyable) because it feels good.
>
> Finally, the behaviour may be designed to communicate the need for **attention**.

Further consideration needs to be given to individual and environmental factors that make the type of communications referred to above more likely to occur (see *Figure 1*, overleaf).

Individual factors

People with learning disabilities may well have specific needs that make them more vulnerable and hence more likely to present challenging behaviour. Some specific syndromes or conditions associated with learning disability have been shown to make challenging behaviour more likely. These include factors such as epilepsy and mental health problems. However, there is a great deal of controversy surrounding this and some authors have suggested that the relationship between these factors and challenging behaviour has been overemphasised. Less controversially, there are clearer links between communication, sensory and physical difficulties and the presentation of challenging behaviour.

Environment factors

When people are placed in environments that fail to meet the types of needs referred to above, it is almost inevitable that challenging behaviour will occur. Unfortunately, research suggests that often services are not well designed and

Figure 1: Factors affecting an individual's challenging behaviour
Adapted from McGill and Toogood (1994)

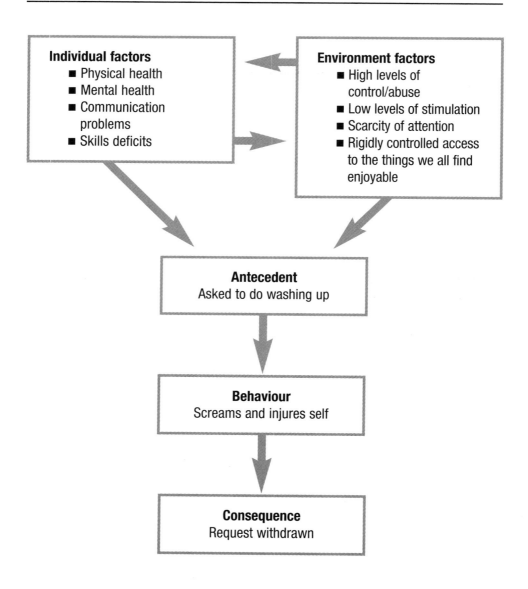

will actively contribute to challenging behaviour. These may be characterised by:

- high levels of control and even abuse
- low levels of stimulation and a scarcity of attention
- rigidly controlled access to the things we all find enjoyable.

An individual with very few things in their life that they like may find themselves having their favourite thing removed, in an attempt to make them behave better. The person labelled 'attention seeking' may be ignored with the assumption that the attention is not needed or deserved.

Responding to challenging behaviour

Traditionally, the most common response to the management of challenging behaviour has been the use of medication. Very few people would argue that medication is the sole answer and some critics would suggest that the use of medication to manage behaviour, when there is no identified mental illness, is unethical. Positive behavioural support is increasingly being recognised as offering the most ethical and effective framework for supporting people with learning disabilities who present challenging behaviour. This approach emphasises the importance of understanding:

- the nature of the message communicated by the behaviour
- the relevant individual factors
- the nature of the individual's environment.

Positive behavioural support equally emphasises the importance of intervening with the person in an ethical and person-centred manner.

Punishment

Most of us were raised with the overt use of punishment; when we were naughty we were reprimanded, had privileges withdrawn or were even smacked. It is, perhaps, understandable that care staff will use experiences of 'parenting-type management' in their work with people with learning disabilities and challenging behaviour.

There are basic differences in the circumstances of normal child-rearing practices and care of people with learning disabilities that make the use of punishment unacceptable. Punishment has not worked thus far for these people – otherwise they would not have reached adulthood and still be presenting challenging behaviour. In addition, the rights of adults are very different from those of children and, in many cases, the use of punishment strategies may be potentially unlawful. Therefore, any intervention needs to take place within a framework that respects the person's dignity and basic human rights.

Interventions

The scope of the intervention should not be limited to bringing about a reduction in the behaviour. There should also be an expectation that the negative impact that the challenging behaviour has on that individual's quality of life should be directly addressed. We should, therefore, be striving to bring about more access to choice and control in the lives of these people, while also encouraging the development of a wider range of meaningful relationships. Given these expectations, and the likelihood that numerous factors will underlie the presentation of the challenging behaviour, interventions will necessarily involve many different elements that alone would be unlikely to be truly effective, but combined should bring about positive change.

Individual factors

The following factors may well be involved in the causation of the individual's challenging behaviour – they all lie within the individual and so the focus of the intervention would be to change that person in some way.

Physical health

If the person is in some degree of discomfort as a result of physical health difficulties, this distress may well be communicated by challenging behaviour, especially if they also have limited communication skills. Naturally, in such situations it would be essential that the person receive the appropriate medical treatment in order to alleviate the discomfort.

Mental health

It is thought that people with learning disabilities are particularly prone to mental health difficulties. Challenging behaviour may well be exhibited as a result and appropriate psychiatric treatment should be offered. However, this is an area that is controversial and there is an argument that the high rates of mental health difficulties may be overstated. Often people are prescribed psychiatric medication simply to tranquillise them even if there are no mental health problems. Clearly such practices are unacceptable.

There is also growing evidence that people with learning disabilities who present challenging behaviour are extremely vulnerable to abuse and may well be traumatised by this. In this case, the individual should have access to psychological help and be provided with safe and supportive environments where hopefully they will learn that such things will not happen again.

Communication problems

Learning disability is often associated with communication problems. This may involve difficulty in expressing and in understanding. These difficulties are closely related to the presence of challenging behaviour, where the behaviour serves as some form of communication. In such situations, efforts designed to increase the individual's communication skills are likely, over time, to influence the occurrence of challenging behaviour.

Skill deficits

The nature of learning disability almost inevitably means that there will be some tasks that individuals cannot do for themselves – making them reliant on carers to meet at least some of their needs or wants. This increases the chances of something going wrong if, for example, nobody is available at the time the person requires assistance or the carer does not understand what the person needs.

This in turn may be associated with the occurrence of challenging behaviour. An obvious positive strategy here would be to teach that person the skills to do things for themselves, so that they are less reliant on those around them to meet their needs or wants.

Inevitably in life there are occasions when we all experience things that are not quite to our liking. More often than not we cope because, although we might feel like having an outburst, we judge that this would actually make the situation worse for us. Some people with learning disabilities may not have acquired ways of coping with life's everyday irritations and may require coping skills to be taught in the same way as we described the teaching of independent living skills.

Environment factors

As stated, if an environment does not meet the needs of the people who live there, those people are likely to protest and may well do this by exhibiting challenging behaviour. Clearly, any efforts designed to make the environment more supportive for those people would be likely to bring about a reduction in challenging behaviour. These mismatches between need and environment will be very individual and require an understanding of the person and their situation. *Table 1* has examples of change in the person's environment that are related to the communication messages highlighted by the assessment.

A list of changes could be introduced that are not related to any of the communication messages above. For example, if it were possible, removing the specific trigger for the behaviour would have an immediate effect on the occurrence of that behaviour. In addition, a theoretically endless list of changes could be introduced in that person's environment that would bring about a reduction in challenging behaviour, ranging from turning down the volume of the television to arranging for the person to move house.

Managing the occurrence of challenging behaviour

All of the strategies in *Table 1* are designed to prevent the challenging behaviour from occurring and, if based on a good understanding of the person and properly implemented, should bring about gradual reduction, over time, in the challenging behaviour. However, there will still need to be plans in place that tell carers what they should do when the behaviour occurs.

Current thinking regarding the management of challenging behaviour states that the **positive prevention strategies** outlined in *Table 1* are essential, and that when planning what to do in response to the behaviour we should be focusing primarily on safety and not be overly concerned with what seems to be rewarding behaviour. This is sometimes difficult for carers to grasp, as it appears to conflict with 'parenting-type management'. However, what is being proposed is that it is the positive prevention strategies that will make the difference in the long term. If the situation involves safety issues then perhaps 'giving in', for example, is good idea if it keeps everybody safe.

A good management plan should contain things that carers can do earlier in a difficult situation to 'nip it in the bud'. These are situations where you have some idea that difficult behaviour might occur. Perhaps you have noticed something in the environment that will typically trigger the behaviour, or the individual is starting to behave in a way that indicates that more serious behaviour is coming. These plans would again be individual and based on strategies that have proven to work for that person and would include things like distraction and calming techniques.

Table 1: Changes that relate to communication messages

Communication message	Changes needed in the environment
Demand avoidance	If **demand avoidance** is a significant message communicated by the person's challenging behaviour, then perhaps serious consideration should be given to altering the amount or type of demands made on the individual. The demands might be reduced in frequency, difficulty or duration in order to make them more acceptable for the individual. In addition, you could try strategies such as behavioural momentum, ie. where the individual is approached and asked to perform tasks with which they are known to be highly likely to co-operate, thus establishing a momentum of co-operation before being asked to perform a more difficult task. Similarly, simply approaching the person and engaging in social 'chit-chat' before asking them to perform a task may well make co-operation more likely.
Tangible reinforcement	Where the message of the challenging behaviour is the need for an object or activity the person likes, ie. **tangible reinforcement**, a straightforward change may be to make these things more freely available for the person in order that they might be able to 'help themselves'. If the person has physical or motor difficulties they may well require items in the environment to be specially adapted in order that they can use them independently. There would be some overlap between skills teaching here, whereby the person may also require some assistance in acquiring the skills to enable them to get things for themselves.
Self-stimulation	If the purpose for the behaviour is **self-stimulation** (doing something for the sensation felt at the time of doing it) it could be assumed that the environment lacks the right type or amount of stimulation for that person. Often people with learning disabilities who have also been labelled autistic have unusual sensory needs or preferences and it would be unlikely that these needs would be met without specific planning.
Attention	Where the person is exhibiting challenging behaviour in order to get **attention**, perhaps the provision of more attention that was not dependent on challenging behaviour might assist in its reduction.

Physical interventions

It is generally recognised that there will be rare occasions that may require carers to physically intervene with the client to prevent injury to the person or to others. In order to be within a sound legal and ethical framework the following principles should be followed.

- A risk assessment of situations where the management of challenging behaviour might involve physical intervention should be carried out in order that all other alternatives have been ruled out.
- Consideration should be given to whether that individual is capable of consenting to the physical intervention. If so, their consent should be sought. If not, and there is no lasting power of attorney, an order made by the Court of Protection or an appointed deputy, wide-ranging consultation should be conducted, including the individual's advocate, relatives, appropriately qualified and experienced professionals, etc.
- If the desired outcome for that individual is a reduction in the frequency, duration or impact of their challenging behaviour, an intervention plan should be devised with the appropriate balance between reactive strategies and prevention.
- An individualised **written** management plan should be constructed, including steps required to prevent the behaviour from either occurring at all or escalating.
- All care staff working with that individual should be trained as a team and be **competent** in the execution of this plan.
- All use of physical intervention should be **recorded**.
- The use of physical intervention should be **reviewed** to ensure that they are not being used to excess, they continue to promote the safety of service users and staff, and only those interventions detailed in the written management plan are being used.

Summary

Understanding the communication, individual and environmental factors underlying an individual's challenging behaviour is a vital requirement in positive behavioural support plans and should not only hope to reduce challenging behaviour, but also achieve a better quality of life for that person. Given the range of influences on the person that lead to the challenging behaviour and the wide range of outcomes expected, interventions should:

- be person-centred and ethical
- address individual and environmental factors
- have many elements
- consider ways to react to the behaviour that will ensure safety and prevent the situation from becoming worse.

Further reading

Allen D (2002) *Behavioural Management in Intellectual Disabilities: Ethical responses to challenging behaviour.* Kidderminster: BILD.

Baker PA, LaVigna GW and Willis TJ (1998) Understanding and responding to challenging behaviour: a multi-element approach. In: W Fraser, D Sines and M Kerr (Eds) *Hallas's Caring for People with Learning Disabilities (9th edition).* Oxford: Butterworth Heinemann.

Emerson E (2001) *Challenging Behaviour: Analysis and intervention in people with learning difficulties (2nd edition).* Cambridge: Cambridge University Press.

Emerson E, McGill P and Mansell J (1994) *Severe Learning Disabilities and Challenging Behaviours: Designing high quality services* pp232–259. London: Chapman and Hall.

Reference

McGill P and Toogood S (1994) Organising community placements. In: E Emerson, P McGill and J Mansell (Eds) *Severe Learning Disabilities and Challenging Behaviours: Designing high quality services.* London: Chapman and Hall.

Chapter 12

Being who you are

Working with people with profound and multiple disabilities

Key words

multiple learning disability, profound learning disability, stigmatise, labels, sensory disabilities, terminology

'We still don't know how to work with them.'
'It's difficult to work with people when you're not getting any feedback.'

These quotes are from participants interviewed as part of a research project reported by Phoebe Caldwell in her book, *Getting in Touch* (1996). Such comments can be typical of those made by people supporting individuals with profound disabilities. For some, there is frustration at not knowing what to do as a worker or what is expected. For others, there may be fear, or even repulsion, in finding oneself face to face with a person who they perceive to be so very different from themselves – perhaps physically as well as intellectually. These feelings need to be acknowledged, as they are likely to obstruct any effective work and will stop the worker from getting to know the individual as a person with his or her unique personality, interests, likes and dislikes.

People with a profound learning disability (PLD) or profound and multiple learning disabilities (PMLD) form a small but significant group within the learning disabled population. It is increasingly recognised that people with PLD or PMLD need specific types of support, likely to differ in nature and intensity from the support needed by individuals with moderate or mild learning disabilities.

This chapter begins by defining profound and profound and multiple disability, and describes some of the key implications for service providers. A case study is used to illustrate ways in which multidisciplinary teams can work collaboratively with service users and their supporters. Emphasis is placed on principles of good practice aimed at minimising the social inclusion experienced by many people with high support needs.

Definitions: who are we talking about?

Before thinking about what support is needed by people with PLD or PMLD, it is important to be clear about the group of people we are talking about. Various labels and terms have been used, including:

- profound disabilities
- profound and multiple disabilities
- high support needs
- complex needs
- complex and multiple disabilities.

All of the above terms may be useful, but the language used must be agreed and used consistently within an organisation or service to avoid confusion. As a starting point for discussion that would take place within local services, some definitions are offered in *Box 1*.

Box 1: Definitions

As mentioned in *Chapter 1*, a 'significant impairment' is indicated by an IQ score of below 70 (the average for the general population is 100).

People with profound learning disabilities would have an estimated IQ in the 'below 20' range – although actual measurement at this level is not possible. People with profound learning disabilities are functioning at the very early stages of development, and have skills that are acquired by 'typically' developing children in the first year of life.

People with profound and multiple learning disabilities experience disabilities *in addition to* their learning disabilities. These may include one or more of the following in any combination: sensory or physical disabilities; mental health problems; autism; challenging or self-injurious behaviour.

Being consistent with language also helps to ensure that the extent of an individual's disability is acknowledged and respected. While labels of any kind have the potential to stigmatise, sensitive use of clear terminology maps out what people need and indicates the types of support that are likely to be required. Unclear and inconsistent use of labelling can put people at risk of receiving inadequately planned support. This can compromise the individual's quality of life and, in some cases, could lead to poor physical and/or psychological health.

Designing services

While general definitions are possible, it is important to note that, like any population, people with profound disabilities form a very diverse group. Support must be designed at a very individual, person-centred level, which is always about knowing people well. Designing effective support consists of thorough assessment of what the person needs, careful planning of support informed by the assessment and a clear method of evaluating the support provided to determine its effectiveness.

In her book, *Person to Person* (1998), Phoebe Caldwell talks about how she begins this process, and its value:

> *'I want to know, as far as possible, how [people with profound disabilities] perceive their world – how it feels to them. Within the parameters of where they feel safe, how can we enlarge and enrich their experience? How can we increase their confidence and help them to "feel good" about themselves and others?'*

Assessment

For people with PLD or PMLD, the nature and complexities of their disabilities mean that a thorough multidisciplinary assessment is essential. Phoebe Caldwell and Pene Stevens, in the film *Creative Conversations* (2005), stress that the starting point of any attempt at getting to know a person must be close and careful observation. In addition, assessment needs to be across professions – from a number of perspectives – with close collaboration and inclusion of the individual and his or her family or carers. A working list of principles is provided in *Box 2* (overleaf).

Planning support

A thorough assessment will produce a wealth of information, and may well identify a number of areas that could be addressed. It may be more practical to identify the most pressing issues and address those, rather than try to meet all of the identified needs at once.

Planning needs to take place within person-centred planning, ensuring that the individual is at the heart of the process and is involved as much as

Box 2: Principles of the assessment process

- Spend time with the person in a range of different settings (eg. at home, in the community and at the day centre). Watch how s/he responds to different people and different situations.
- Try to establish how the person shows like or dislike.
- Support and participate in the completion of standardised assessment tools used by professionals from the local community team. These tools are used to assess areas such as the individual's communication skills, their vision and hearing abilities or their level of social functioning. Many of these require information from informants other than the service user – give careful thought as to who the most appropriate informants might be.
- Consult with the individual's GP or the local community learning disability nurse and ask for a health assessment to be completed (eg. the 'OK Health Check').
- Spend time getting to know the individual's family and/or significant others. Respect for the individual's personal history is a key element of good practice.
- Observe the individual's personal relationships, and the extent to which they seem *meaningful* to him or her.

possible (see **Chapter 7**). Decision-making about the design of the person's support is likely to take place in a meeting, which can easily exclude the person and sometimes any relatives attending. Some useful pointers for ensuring that meetings, and the rest of the planning process, remain person-centred are listed in **Box 3**.

A useful form of person-centred planning that is felt to be effective for people with profound disabilities is essential lifestyle planning. This is a way of establishing what is 'essential' to the individual and helps record how s/he communicates likes and dislikes. People in the group supporting the individual might ask themselves a number of key questions and come to some consensus as to what might be true for the person. For example, the following questions might be useful to ask.

- What would a 'good' day be like for this person?
- What would a 'bad' day be like?
- What do we think makes him/her happy?
- What do we think makes him/her sad?
- What do we need to know/do to support this person?

Box 3: Good practice in planning with people with profound and multiple learning disabilities

- Consider whether attending part, or all, of the meeting will be meaningful for the person.
- Think carefully about who should attend. Has the individual met all of the participants before? If not, why are they there?
- Collect information with and about the person that can be shared at the meeting (eg. video of being involved in favourite activities, holiday photographs etc).
- Consider the venue and time of day carefully. Is this a room where the individual feels comfortable? Is there optimal lighting if they have a visual impairment? Are they likely to make other associations with the function of the room (eg. the room is used for dinner or physiotherapy)? Is the meeting straight after lunch when the individual might feel sleepy?
- Consult with the local speech and language therapist to ensure that any appropriate communication aids are available to the person.

During the meeting

- Make the individual's involvement the focal point of the meeting. Use photographs, video footage, scrapbooks and sensory and other objects to prompt discussion and encourage the individual to respond.
- Avoid talking over his or her head – refer conversation back, maintain eye contact and use visual prompts or objects of reference to indicate what is being discussed.
- Make sure that the meeting remains focused and does not go on too long.
- Ensure that the meeting is positive – focus on strengths, interests and areas for development, rather than a list of what the person 'cannot do' or problem behaviours.
- Keep it positive – try to keep challenging behaviour and health-related issues to separate meetings unless they have direct relevance for the decision being made.
- Make sure that family members and/or advocates are given a central role to any decision-making.

After the meeting

- Make sure action points are translated into practice and do not get lost.
- Reflect on what happened during the meeting with other participants. Could things have been done differently? What have we learned about how the individual participates that might help us to enhance their participation next time?

Evaluating interventions

The ways we support people with profound disabilities and our interventions need to be evaluated to check that they are achieving what was intended. This can be done in a number of ways, but will need to be tied directly to the nature of the support being provided. Examples of measures used to evaluate interventions include:

- a rating scale completed by staff to monitor an individual's reaction when offered a new activity
- a graph to plot, for example, the frequency of head-banging before and after an intervention, which aims to engage the individual in alternative behaviours
- a questionnaire administered to family members seeking to establish their perception of an individual's reaction to a new short break service.

The case study opposite demonstrates an approach to understanding Sofia's world that has several themes.

- Assessment is concerned with Sofia's relationships and how she interacts with her world.
- Her developmental level and interests are placed at the centre of any planning of support.
- Everybody that knows Sofia well is involved and their perspectives are valued.
- Interventions build on her interests and advocate one-to-one time and support as good practice.

A developmental approach to support

Providing effective support for people with PLD or PMLD requires a collaborative approach that is developmentally appropriate for the individual concerned. Some find this approach difficult, as they feel that it compromises the individual's dignity and right to be respected as an adult.

However, the increasing evidence base emerging to support the use of developmental approaches (see **Further reading** at the end of this chapter), suggests that acknowledging an individual's level of functioning is essential if we are to support their development, enhance their engagement and encourage them to form meaningful relationships with other people. If handled sensitively, it can be argued that adopting a developmental approach is the clearest way of showing respect for an individual.

Case study: Sofia

Sofia is 21 and lives with her parents. She has profound learning disabilities, uses a wheelchair and wears strong glasses. The community nurse working with Sofia noticed that she had started becoming very withdrawn, not maintaining eye contact and refusing to eat. Staff at Sofia's day centre had also noticed that she had stopped being as vocal and was engaging in self-involved behaviour (repeatedly playing with her fingers). Sofia's community nurse decided to instigate a multidisciplinary assessment. This involved the speech and language therapist, the clinical psychologist, Sofia's parents, the occupational therapist and staff at Sofia's day centre. The process consisted of assessing:

- social functioning – conducted by the clinical psychologist in consultation with Sofia's parents
- Sofia's activity programme – conducted by the occupational therapist
- interview with the day centre staff
- observation of Sofia both at home and at the day centre.

Information from the assessments was collated and a planning meeting held. Sofia attended for part of the meeting – her keyworker from the day centre supported her to show video footage of Sofia taking part in activities, while her parents played an audio tape of Sofia singing along to songs with her mother.

The meeting agreed that evidence from the assessment suggested that Sofia was functioning in the early stages of development and would need a significant amount of one-to-one time to make sense of her environment. It was also observed that such support was not readily available during the day and Sofia was finding it difficult to participate in activities. She was often in groups of three people or more, most of whom were more assertive than her. This was perhaps leading to feelings of being out of control and ultimately to depression – a possible explanation for her reluctance to eat.

A plan was drawn up, which built in one-to-one sessions, providing Sofia with opportunities for developing relationships and engaging in meaningful activities. These activities were designed to build on Sofia's apparent interest in music (ie. singing songs) and provide her with opportunities for interacting at her own pace.

Three months after the planning meeting, a review of the intervention was held. Video footage was shown of Sofia working with staff at the centre and community team members. Supporters encouraged Sofia to take part in turn-taking exchanges, singing her favourite songs and playing musical instruments. This work was **developmentally appropriate*** in that it focused on Sofia's skills and encouraged her to interact at her own pace and on her own initiative. The video suggested that when Sofia was interacting in this way, she tended to not spend time playing with her fingers and was able to increase her eye contact with her interactive partner.

*Based on the principles of **intensive interaction** – see under **Further reading**.

Summary

People with PLD or PMLD can be at risk of social exclusion and services should work collaboratively across professional disciplines, and with carers and families, to plan effective support with and for individuals. Taking a developmental approach within a thorough assessment process helps to ensure that any intervention is person-centred. Highly individualised support that is regularly evaluated can provide people with PLD or PMLD with an acceptable quality of life that consists of much more than just having physical needs met. Innovative and creative thinking between people who know the individual well can lead to the support of a lifestyle based on autonomy, choice and meaningful relationships.

Further reading

Caldwell P (2002) *Learning the Language*. Brighton: Pavilion Publishing (Brighton) Ltd.

Lacey P and Ouvray C (1998) *People with Profound and Multiple Learning Disabilities: A collaborative approach to meeting complex needs*. London: David Fulton.

Nind M and Hewett D (2001) *Intensive Interaction: A practice guide*. London: BILD.

Ware J (1996) *Creating Responsive Environments for People with Profound and Multiple Learning Disabilities*. London: David Fulton.

The PMLD network: www.pmldnetwork.org
A forum site maintained by the Foundation for People with Learning Disabilities.

References

Caldwell P (1996) *Getting in Touch*. Brighton: Pavilion Publishing (Brighton) Ltd.

Caldwell P (2005) *Creative Conversations*. Brighton: Pavilion Publishing (Brighton) Ltd.

Caldwell P with Stevens P (1998) *Person to Person*. Brighton: Pavilion Publishing (Brighton) Ltd.

Chapter 13

Taking the strain

Mental health and people with learning disabilities

Key words

distress, mental health, mental illness, positive evaluation, predisposing factors, well-being

Health is a state of physical and emotional well-being. All of us have times of illness, either physical or mental. When a person is mentally ill, his or her mind does not function as it usually does. That person's thoughts, emotions, beliefs or ability to reason change and behaviour is 'out of character'.

People from different cultures believe and do different things. When someone has a mental illness, his or her behaviour differs from the usual pattern and may stand out as different to those of other people from the same culture.

Factors underpinning mental ill health

Mental ill health is common. We all react differently to particular stresses, depending on our genetic make up and life experiences. Mental ill health is more common in people with learning disabilities – this is probably because they are more likely to have a number of predisposing factors. These factors are listed in *Box 1* (overleaf).

Some of these risk factors can be reduced. For example, we might try to promote positive mental health by improving people's self-esteem in the way we treat them, teaching them ways to cope with stress (eg. relaxation) or by increasing their ability to communicate (eg. by using non-verbal means).

Box 1: Predisposing factors for mental ill health in people with learning disabilities

Genetic, some kinds of mental illness tend to run in families, eg. mood disorders, such as depression, and some genetic conditions are associated with an increased risk of particular mental health problems, eg. people with Down's syndrome are at increased risk of developing Alzheimer's dementia

Adverse environmental conditions, these include social isolation, abuse and bullying

Sensory impairments, for example, hearing difficulties and communication difficulties

Physical ill health, itself can increase the risk of developing mental ill health, as can certain medications, including some given to treat epilepsy

Brain damage

Note: These risk factors can affect us all, but are more common in those with learning disabilities. Also, more than one of these factors may act together at any given time.

Case study

Two nursing colleagues facilitated a mental health promotion group being run as a series of workshops. The group was evaluated positively by those attending. It helped service users to recognise when they are stressed and to develop coping strategies for stress. They became more aware of mental ill health, especially depression and anxiety. The workshops also provided service users with information regarding the range of services available in their borough, not only clinical services, but also leisure, advocacy and support services.

Issues in assessment and diagnosis

It is often difficult to put feelings into words. People with autism find this especially hard (see *Chapter 9*), as do those with limited communication skills (see *Chapter 6*). People with mental illness may not be able to describe or understand what is happening to them. We need to be alert to a change in a person's demeanour and behaviour. Such changes may be due to ill health, either mental or physical, and need treatment. People with learning disabilities may need support to access help. A GP may be able to offer advice and treatment, put the person in contact with a self-help group or make a referral to a specialist service, such as to a counsellor, psychologist or psychiatrist.

Clearly, an individual's behaviour can change for lots of reasons not to do with ill health. People with a mental health problem are often feared or disliked because of the negative emotions that the label 'mental illness' produces. This is prejudice. We can all become mentally ill and it is very common. A person with learning disabilities has often suffered prejudice already and becoming mentally ill can be seen as another damaging label. We need to support the person with learning disabilities appropriately and this requires an open mind. The possibility of mental ill health should be considered as one of a number of reasons why a person seems to be 'not him or herself'. If I seem a bit low and off my food it may be that I've gone on a diet and I am missing my food! It may also be because I don't like what I'm being offered, or that I have a bug or am depressed. There are many possibilities. Only by looking at the whole picture can we start to understand what is going on.

Box 2: Possible signs of mental ill health

When people with learning disabilities develop mental ill health, families/carers may notice:

- changes in sleep pattern, appetite and loss of interest in usual activities
- mood changes including irritability, anxiety or they may become fearful
- behaviour change such as if a person who is normally friendly becomes withdrawn or aggressive
- inability to carry out tasks that are normal for that person.

Case study: Susan

Even quite unusual behaviours can have mundane causes. Susan was increasingly distressed and aggressive. She has no verbal communication, and it was difficult to understand why she was so different to her usual self. She was also off her food and losing weight. There had been no recent changes in the people around her, or her routines. Careful examination revealed the need for extensive dental work. Once this was done she returned to her usual self.

People who support those with learning disabilities are vital in alerting professionals to the possibility of a mental health problem. Their knowledge will clarify the change in a person's mood, thinking and behaviour. They can support a person to seek specialist advice. This is especially important when a person has limited communication skills. They can also assist in monitoring the effect of treatment. We need to know if an intervention is not working or is having unwanted effects, so that appropriate action is taken. Sometimes support staff may be asked to complete simple charts to help in this process.

Case study: James

I was asked to see James by his GP. James left school a year ago. Since then he had become increasingly sullen and bad tempered at home. He was not interested in doing things, such as playing his music. When I talked to James, he told me he was unhappy because he couldn't get a job or a girlfriend like other men his age. He felt his family did not understand him. I thought that James needed someone to talk his problems through with, and he agreed to see a counsellor. Together, they discussed how James might get closer to achieving what he wanted.

One day I was called to see James urgently as he had hit his mother for no apparent reason. He was very distressed, and unable to explain why he had done this. He then said he was hearing clicking in his head. I could not find a physical reason for this. I started James, with his agreement, on some tablets to remove what I supposed were hallucinations (clicking). Soon James was back to his usual self. He started some courses and began to see old friends again. James and I decided to see if he could manage without his tablets. Unfortunately, James began to feel miserable again and to hear 'noises in his head'. He asked to restart his tablets. We agreed to try to stop them again when he has been well for a year.

James continues to see a counsellor to find ways to be more positive in the way he thinks about himself and his changing role from that of a child to a more independent adult living in the family home. The help James is receiving aims to make him feel better and to cope differently in the future so that he is less likely to become ill again.

James was more ill than I had at first thought. I had viewed him as a young man understandably upset by what he saw as his lack of opportunities. Only later did I realise the depth of his distress, and that he was hearing sounds that no one else could (hallucinations of clicking). When a person becomes mentally ill, normal feelings and thoughts may become more intense than usual and interfere with how they cope. This is what happens when someone has a neurotic disorder. I thought that James's sadness had reached this stage, and that he was neurotically depressed. Later I realised that James was, to a degree, out of touch with reality – he was having hallucinations – which is referred to as a psychotic illness.

There is no clear boundary between mental health and mental illness, or between neuroses and psychoses. There are many shades of grey in between, and of course our health changes from day to day. The approach we take to help a person depends on many things.

Treatment

Throughout, James and I have talked about what we should do. It is important for all of us to give 'informed consent' to any treatment we have. This means that we understand what the treatment is and what the effects of it might be. We also need to know what is likely to happen if we do not have the treatment. This does not only apply to medicines but also to other treatments, such as relaxation and counselling. James and I could talk together. It is more difficult to gain the view of someone with less verbal skills. However, wherever possible a service user's consent to treatment should be sought. There are special procedures that need to be followed if this cannot happen, which your organisation will have, to comply with the Mental Capacity Act (2005).

There are a variety of treatments available including different psychotherapies, medicines, relaxation and behavioural strategies. For James, a combination of counselling and medicine has worked well. For someone else, a different approach may be better.

There are times when a person with learning disabilities who becomes mentally ill will need to be in hospital for treatment. This may be because the doctors and nurses want to keep a closer watch and provide a safe environment. This does not happen often, as most people will receive treatment at home. The length of time spent in hospital varies from person to person depending on other needs, such as medical and social support.

Case study: Helen

Helen lives with her mother and attends college regularly. She suddenly became frightened as she was seeing people that do not actually exist (visual hallucinations) in her room. She was worried they may want to harm her. Sometimes, she would scream and would not go to sleep at night. Helen's mother could not understand what had happened and could not cope with looking after her. Helen was admitted to hospital and, after some blood tests, doctors found that she had a serious medical problem, as her thyroid gland was not functioning properly. As soon as the thyroid problem was corrected, Helen became her usual self and went back after four weeks to live with her mother.

Summary

Those who support people with learning disabilities need to:

- promote positive mental health, for example by promoting relationships and active lifestyles
- be alert to the possibility that if a person is not their normal self there could be a variety of reasons, including mental illness
- be able to support people to access help
- assist in the implementation of treatments
- be able to monitor the effects of interventions
- assist in re-establishing usual routines including getting back to work and contacting friends and relatives after recovery from a mental ill health problem.

Only by working together can the mental health needs of people with learning disabilities be met.

Acknowledgement

We would like to thank Peter Cronin and the Tuesday Group for their help in revising an earlier version of this chapter.

Further reading

Bouras N (1999) (Ed) *Psychiatric and Behavioural Disorders in Developmental Disabilities and Mental Retardation*. Cambridge: Cambridge Press.

Hollins S and Curran J (1996) *Understanding Depression in People with Learning Disabilities: A training pack for staff and carers*. Brighton: Pavilion Publishing (Brighton) Ltd.

Holt G, Hardy S and Bouras N (2006) *Mental Health in Learning Disabilities: A reader*. Brighton: Pavilion Publishing (Brighton) Ltd.

Department of Constitutional Affairs (2005) *Mental Capacity Act*. London: Her Majesty's Stationery Office.

O'Hara J and Sperlinger A (1997) Mental health needs. In: J O'Hara and A Sperlinger (Eds) *Learning Disabilities: A practical approach for health professionals*. Chichester: Wileys.

Piachaud J (1999) Issues for mental health in learning disabilities services. *Tizard Learning Disability Review* **4** (2) 47–48.

Part three

Shaping lives together

Chapter 14

It's not what you know, it's who

Enabling and supporting community involvement

Key words
community, connections, relationships, social inclusion

What is it that makes you feel a part of a community? Any community – whether it's where you live, your work, sports club, political group, religious group or one of the numerous other communities you probably relate to. Take a moment to think about it.

Done? Our bet is that you may have come up with words or phrases like *'friends', 'a sense of belonging', 'similar interests', 'shared beliefs and goals', 'common experiences', 'having fun together', 'knowing people'* and *'making a contribution that's valued'*. Most, if not all, will reflect some form of interaction and unity between you and other people – because, essentially, that's what feeling a part of a community is all about. Even the most modern communities – in cyberspace – are all about people interacting with each other.

So, if feeling part of a community – feeling involved – is about relationships and interaction, then a key task for people supporting citizens with learning difficulties has to be to deliberately build their connections with others. In this chapter we explore why building community connections and involvement is so crucial, and offer some ideas about how to go about it.

But, what does 'community' mean?

This is an important question – the King's Fund provided guidance in 1988:

> *'The best way we have found of thinking about community is to imagine it as the set of ties and connections which a person has with others'.*

There's clearly a dilemma when thinking about people who spend a great deal of their time in segregated settings (like village communities, long-stay hospitals or day centres). Are we advocating that individuals be supported to build 'ties and connections' with other disabled people in segregated communities? In part, we are. At a personal level, having friends around us day to day enhances our lives. Disabled people have shared experiences and issues – a 'community of interest' – which is the basis for development of advocacy and pressure groups. Enabling people with learning difficulties to come together to enjoy each other's company and to gain strength from each other is positive and desirable. *But*, building community connections and involvement is, and must be, about more than that.

We have to look beyond the community of disabled people. If we don't, we fail people, we fail ourselves, and we fail society. In 1992 John O'Brien and Connie Lyle O'Brien wrote:

> *'exclusion decreases the human diversity that can energise civic life, with obvious cost to people with severe disabilities and their families'.*

It is fundamentally a moral issue about the kind of society we want to live in.

> *'Segregation is the offspring of an illicit intercourse between injustice and immorality.'* (Martin Luther King, Jr)

Steve Dowson, exploring the meaning of community (1995) describes a *'personal community – a matrix of people, places, and roles, unique to each individual'*, which *'provides not only a sense of identity for the person, but actual identity in the eyes of others'*. Thus, building connections beyond the community of disabled people gives people identity in society. It demonstrates people's status as citizens. It opens the door to more friendships and to informal, natural support. But, as he points out, what is really important is that people are helped to build connections and involvement in their local area – with their neighbourhood community. It is interaction with local people that can give a real sense of belonging.

Supporting people to get involved in their neighbourhood community also recognises that people with learning difficulties have something to offer others. Amitai Etzioni (2000) states that *'mutuality is central to communities. A good society relies even more on mutuality – people helping each other rather than merely helping those in need'*.

With citizenship rights go responsibilities. People with learning difficulties share a responsibility to contribute to the development of a 'good society'. Building ordinary community connections provides the opportunity for people to step out of a dependency role and give something to their local community and society.

Does involvement really matter?

Isolation and loneliness are big social problems and it is clear from research that most people with learning difficulties have very limited social networks, which makes loneliness more likely (Bayley, 1997). Being an active participant in a number of communities makes life enjoyable and stimulating. *Feeling* involved and a part of things can help give us a sense of worth and purpose and, ultimately, it may help prevent mental health problems. Many people with learning difficulties have lives that revolve around the services they attend and their family. Their contact with local people is through, or mediated by, their parents or staff. They do not themselves have reciprocal relationships with people other than family. As their close family declines they are in danger of becoming even more bereft of the warmth and joy that reciprocal relationships with others bring. It is essential that services recognise this and do things to help people build a range of relationships and connections now.

For people from ethnic minorities, involvement with their own cultural community can help to overcome feelings of difference and fears of prejudice or rejection (Baxter *et al*, 1990).

Case study: Halil

For Halil, a Turkish Cypriot in London, one of the most important things about being supported to go to the gym every week is that he often sees a woman there who speaks Turkish with him. He loves going to a local cafe run by Turkish Cypriot people because he feels at home, but the community day service doesn't support him to go there often. He is disappointed that there are no staff supporting him who share his culture or language. Halil feels there is a gap in his life and wants to do more alongside other Turkish Cypriot people. Being involved with his own community really matters to him.

Being connected and involved with other people is indeed important – it's what makes life worth living. Communities are about people and the greater their – our – involvement and contribution, the more a community benefits.

How do we build people's connections and involvement?

There is no single way, so take a flexible, multi-pronged approach. The following approaches can help people to feel included in their community.

Build circles of support

Assist someone to bring a group of people together to help improve their life and realise their goals and dreams. Help them identify people they have a close, reciprocal bond with, others they want to get to know better or who show a genuine interest in them. If someone has limited networks, you may need to engineer and facilitate membership of their circle – laying the foundation for natural relationships to develop in the longer term.

Do things consciously and deliberately

For most of us, community connections and involvement develop naturally during the normal course of daily life. This does not necessarily happen for people with learning difficulties, so it is important to deliberately plan a course of action that aims to achieve that goal. This is one of the paradoxes of the work. You very often have to do something specially planned – something that might seem artificial – in order to achieve something natural. In this case, create new bonds of friendship between people.

Support people to be in the community

Being physically in the community makes it easier for people to develop their connections and involvement, so help people to live in ordinary homes in ordinary streets, use public facilities, get jobs, go to college – it's the best starting point. Lots of us make friends or start relationships, for example, through our work. (See Cathy's case study, opposite.)

Make sure it continues

Like us, you've probably come across many people who have ended their involvement in something they enjoyed, and consequently lost touch with people, because their service changed – their support worker left, a policy changed, money became tight, or they may have had to move away from

Case study: Cathy

There are three people at the heart of Cathy's circle: her mum, her keyworker from the residential home where she lives, and a woman called Jenny. Cathy met Jenny through her work in an elderly person's home. They work alongside each other and have developed a close bond. Jenny rarely misses any of Cathy's circle meetings and they now exchange cards and gifts as well. With careful nurturing, their friendship has the potential to grow and flourish beyond the workplace.

Case study: Julie

Julie lives in Liverpool. Soon after leaving school she was supported to move from a special needs unit in a day centre to take up a youth training scheme work placement with the electricity board. She initially received on-the-job support from a supported employment worker, but eventually one of her work colleagues took over. She made a lot of new friends, and when there was a reorganisation at work it was her colleagues who designed a new job for her so that she still had a role. On her 21st birthday Julie had a party packed with friends, family and workmates.

The policy was that youth training placements could only last two years and at the end of that time Julie returned to the day centre. Involvement with her work friends tailed off. Julie went from being a 'workmate' to a 'service user', from an integrated community to a segregated one again. The benefits that Julie had got from youth training were not sustained.

their home. People's community connections and involvement are often at the mercy of the services and support they receive and this is one of the greatest threats. Being conscious of this is the starting point; taking positive action to sustain people's involvement while everything around them may be changing is the challenge. (See Julie's case study, above.)

Know the community

To develop connections and involvement you need to know about the community – whether a neighbourhood, work community, or any other type of community. Where do people pass the time of day? Who are the socialites and where do people go to socialise? Who could do with some support? Who is interested in what? There are two options: either you get to know the community yourself, or you seek out someone in that community (for example, a key resident: the Dot Cotton of the street!)

to help. The latter is particularly important where you are trying to build someone's connections with an ethnic minority community but you are not, yourself, from that community.

Do things that benefit the whole community

'What is not good for the hive is not good for the bee.' (Marcus Aurelius)

Another way of thinking about this is that supporting someone to do something good for the community will also be good for the person in their own right. Taking a community development approach is about helping people with learning difficulties to contribute something for the benefit of all. It means finding out what the community is missing, or would like to have, and then taking the lead in developing it. For example, setting up a local exchange trading scheme (LETS) would enable people to contribute to their neighbourhood community on an equal basis, at the same time as getting to know local people much better. Community development undertaken in partnership with other members of that community can forge connections and a shared purpose. It creates a sense of belonging. It is important, though, that it is the person with learning difficulties that gets the sense of belonging, not you. Any development must be about you supporting and facilitating – doing things with the person rather than taking over as their main link with other people.

One of the things that makes community involvement more difficult for people with learning difficulties, particularly if they have mobility problems, visual impairments or live in rural areas, is access to public buildings and good transport. This can also be a problem for many other people too, such as young parents with pushchairs and elderly people. Initiating or joining a campaign to improve community transport and access is just one example of action that might benefit the whole community.

Reflect on and change what you do

John and Connie O'Brien (1992) challenge staff and services to actively encourage community involvement, to prioritise people's relationships, contacts and memberships and organise flexibly around them. They challenge staff to be conscious of their own power:

'Service staff could reduce barriers… if they stopped acting as if they own the people they serve and could arbitrarily terminate their contacts or disrupt their memberships.'

Again, the requirement is to act consciously. Building community connections and involvement needs to be 'live' in your mind so that opportunities are recognised and grasped.

Case study: Bola

Bola is a young black woman living in an area where the majority of the people are white. She has no friends who share her ethnic background. Bola was with Amy, a project worker, when they met another young black woman working at the office reception. It soon became clear that the woman recognised Bola from around the village and they struck up a conversation. The woman finished the conversation by saying how nice it was to meet Bola and hopefully they would meet again. And that's how it was left. Later, Amy kicked herself for not having supported Bola to make an arrangement, there and then, to meet the woman again. It was now much more difficult to do, without her name, address or phone number.

Local, regular and targeted

It's not enough just to support people to be in the community. It's what you do that makes the difference when it comes to achieving real involvement. Many day services, for example, arrange regular trips and 'outings' as part of their programme of activities. These *'can give people a good experience but do little to build people's involvement in, or sense of belonging to their community'* (Lloyd & Cole, 2000). Doing things locally means that people are more likely to bump into each other beyond services and there's more chance they will build a connection.

Case study: Jack

Jack and a few others are supported by their day service to go out for a pub lunch every Wednesday. They have been going to the same pub each week for many months so they are now known by the staff and other regulars. Jack feels comfortable and at home in the pub.

It sounds like there's a good foundation to build on – until we consider that the pub is actually 35 miles away from where Jack and his friends live. They can't get there on their own and the chances of them ever seeing people from the pub when they are not using the day service are very slim indeed.

Going to the same local places and doing the same activities regularly, like a weekly slimming group, running club or evening class – where people share a goal or passion – is more likely to result in sustainable connections than going at ad hoc times.

Think carefully about the best places and circumstances for meeting people. It may not be the gym (a fairly solitary activity) unless there's also a bar or cafe where people tend to gather after their workout. Is it a place where people stay around with time to relax, or a more 'transitory' venue with people just passing through? Choose activities carefully with connections in mind. People are more likely to build links with others if they share something in common. It is essential that you know the person well – their interests, preferences, talents and worries. Then you can target your efforts on activities, places and people that have the potential to enhance the person's life. Don't forget that a lot of community life and networks revolve around children. Help people make links with families.

Support people to stay in touch

Supporting people to keep in touch with family, friends and new acquaintances can take effort, especially if people live a long way away. You may need to help someone make a phone call, send postcards, photos, birthday cards or invitations – small but important actions that 'oil the wheels' of relationships.

Case study: Jonathan

Jonathan moved back to his local area from hospital in the early 1990s. He had no contact with his family, used a wheelchair, had little speech and little was known about his interests, likes and dislikes. He went out infrequently – hostel staff were anxious because he would scream and bang his head – until he was specifically linked to two support workers to go out with him on different days of the week.

Jonathan clearly liked being out, even in bad weather, but it was really hard to get a sense of other things he liked to do. 'Going out' was in danger of losing its purpose. The workers therefore visited the hospital to try to get some information about things he had done before or interests he may have had. The visit gave them few clues about his interests, but they did find out that Jonathan had a friend, Paul, who had also moved back to the local area from hospital. The workers arranged for the two to meet up. It went well and Paul indicated that he'd like to see Jonathan regularly. Jonathan and Paul were helped to rekindle their friendship and then to develop a shared interest in tropical fish. Jonathan's life took a turn for the better.

Help the public to open the door

It's still very common to hear people saying that they 'couldn't' support people with learning difficulties, and that they admire people who do. The shame is that many members of the public simply have not been used to having people with learning difficulties participate alongside them. When it happens, people soon overcome their preconceived ideas and fears, begin to feel comfortable and grow in confidence. It is about familiarity and learning, leading to the development of what John McKnight calls *'authentic citizen communities of care'* (1995).

We have a role to play in helping members of the community build their confidence and capacity to welcome people with learning difficulties. It's about paving the way – a worker accompanying someone with their potential new friend so they gain confidence with each other, or working with staff in sports centres, cinemas, or clubs, so they gain an understanding of an individual with learning difficulties who will be joining them.

Case study: Stephen

Stephen lives in an area where bowling is an important sport and social activity. He was really keen to join the bowling club in his village but the club committee was concerned that he would not know how to play and would spoil other people's enjoyment and said no. A worker went to see the chair of the committee and explained that Stephen just needed someone to teach him. As a result a couple came forward and said they would help Stephen. He was signed up as a member of the club and began to play bowls with them regularly.

Emphasise what people can contribute

Supporting people to take on a role – as a good neighbour, a loving uncle, a handy-person – helps others to see them as equal. It reinforces citizenship and makes a positive contribution to community life. It is easier to help someone get involved in a community if they are seen as having something to offer rather than as needing something.

Contributing something may be about a person in a wheelchair lining up alongside local parents and older people to campaign for better access, or joining the horticultural society and growing vegetables on an allotment for the local farmers' market. Someone with limited mobility and no speech can still hand out hymnbooks at a church service or smile a welcome to people attending a football supporters' club meeting. There are so many different ways that people can contribute to their local community. We just

Case study: Ivan

Ivan was clear that he wanted to get involved with a local drama group. He loves acting and has done some television work in the past. His parents are both in the business. People in Ivan's planning circle enthusiastically approached some local groups but found the initial responses very disappointing. People were close to giving up. The breakthrough came when people changed what they said when contacting a group. Instead of talking about Ivan's disability, they focused on what he could do to help the group – the talents he had to offer and the contribution he could make. Ivan joined a group, was soon written into their next production and rehearsing two evenings a week. He was over the moon and made several new contacts in his local community.

need to focus on people's talents and gifts and use our creative and imaginative thinking.

Network, network, network

Building connections and involvement is partly about what you know and what you do, but it's also a lot about who you know and how you use your own, and other people's, networks. If you don't know anyone in the horticultural society, your neighbour might; if you don't know a regular supporter of the local football team, your milkman might. Don't be afraid to ask people for help and ideas. You might get a few rejections along the way, but you're more likely to get some good leads and new ideas.

It's about you and me

As John O'Brien wrote in 1989:

> 'Developing high quality human services… calls for reallocation of service resources, working outside traditional boundaries, and renegotiation of the service's position in community life. This essential work calls for the motivation arising from a vision of inclusive community.'

As ordinary citizens, we want to be involved with communities where people with learning difficulties have a place and take an active part. We want to run into people as friends, at the library, the allotment, the bus stop; we want to see people as colleagues at work, on committees, in action groups; we want to share experiences with people as students, worshippers, neighbours. We believe that inclusion strengthens communities and society and that we therefore have a responsibility, beyond our work, to do things that help to achieve this.

Community inclusion is about what we do in our own lives. What do you do in yours?

This piece first appeared in *Living WELL* (2000) Volume 1 Issue 1, published by Pavilion Journals (Brighton) Ltd. *Living WELL* has been relaunched and is now called *Learning Disability Today.*

References

Bayley M (1997) *What Price Friendship?* Minehead: Hexagon Publishers.

Baxter C, Poonia K, Ward L and Nadirshaw Z (1990) *Double Discrimination: Issues and services for people with learning difficulties from black and ethnic minority communities.* London: King's Fund.

Dowson S (1995) What do we mean by 'community'? *Community Living* **8** (3) 6–7.

Etzioni A (2000) The road to the good society. *New Statesman* (May issue) 25–27.

King's Fund (1998) *Ties and Connections: An ordinary community life for people with learning difficulties.* London: King's Fund.

Lloyd A and Cole A (2001) Building positive lifestyles: the community option. In: C Clark (Ed) *Adult Day Services and Social Exclusion: Better days.* London: Jessica Kingsley Publishers.

McKnight JL (1995) *The Careless Society: Community and its counterfeits.* New York: Basic Books.

O'Brien J (1989) *What's Worth Working For?* Leadership for better quality human services. Lithonia, Georgia: Responsive Systems Associates.

O'Brien J and O'Brien CL (1992) Members of each other: perspectives on social support for people with severe disabilities. In: J Nisbet (Ed) *Natural Supports in School, at Work, and in the Community for People with Severe Disabilities.* Baltimore: Paul Brookes Publishing.

Chapter 15

'I choose – I choose my staff, I choose where I go'

Living with direct payments

Key words
capacity, responsibilities, flexibility, individualisation, participation, control

In this chapter, Karen Slater and her mother, Catherine, share their experiences of using direct payments and describe ways in which this approach to paying for support has affected their lives. Andrew Carpenter sets the scene and provides helpful context for understanding the extent to which this scheme is changing the lives of many people with learning disabilities.

Understanding direct payments

What are direct payments?

Direct payments (DPs) provide people who have been assessed as needing social care services with cash to purchase and arrange their own services. The scheme was set out in the Community Care (Direct Payments) Act 1996, implemented in April 1997.

Who can receive a DP?

- Disabled people aged over 16 (disabled people are defined as people with any kind of impairment and people disabled by illness, such as HIV/Aids)

- People with a parental responsibility for a disabled child
- Carers

Who is eligible for a DP and how do you consent to having one?

To be eligible for a DP someone must have been assessed as needing social care services. They must also be able to indicate preferences and make choices (and therefore consent to having a DP) and be able to manage the DP, although someone can have as much help as is necessary to enable them to do this.

Capacity to make choices and to manage can be in question when it comes to someone with a learning disability. However, the Department of Health guidance (2004) states:

- *'The approach should start from the point of view that a person can consent and then seek to find the evidence to support that.'*
- *'Managing the DP does not have to be something you do yourself, but it does have to produce the outcomes you have chosen.'*
- *'The ability to direct is more important than the ability to manage.'*

In practice, this means that the notion of 'implied consent' to a DP is acceptable and steps should be taken to discover how someone communicates and indicates preference. It is therefore possible to consent to having a DP without fully understanding the paperwork involved.

Capacity to manage a DP

There is paperwork involved in having a DP and the individual with learning disabilities needs to keep records of expenditure and declare these to the local authority at regular intervals (usually quarterly). As the individual will also be directly employing their own workers, they must have what is called 'legal competence' to be an employer, ie. they must have the mental capacity to be an employer.

Where there is doubt about capacity, there are still ways to provide a DP. This may be through using another person as an agent to manage the paperwork on behalf of the individual with learning disabilities. This might be by setting up a User-controlled (or Independent Living) Trust, which means that more than one individual will create a legal trust through a solicitor to act as the employer on behalf of the individual with learning disabilities. Alternatively, some local authorities are using brokers, who will often hold the bank account on someone's behalf, arrange payment for the workers and manage all the paperwork.

What can be bought with a DP?

Any service the individual with learning disabilities (or those with parental responsibility or carer) has been assessed as needing with the exception of permanent residential care. Examples include:

- personal assistance
- day services
- short-term breaks
- mixed packages
- live-in care
- one-off payments to purchase equipment.

What can DPs NOT purchase?

- Permanent residential care
- Local authority services
- Health services
- Services provided by a relative ordinarily living in the same household

How much money will a DP be?

The amount of a DP is determined by the local authority and is usually given as an hourly rate. Local authorities are required to pay a rate that represents a reasonable cost and enables the disabled person to secure the assessed services.

Any DP rate should include enough for:

- employers' national insurance
- employers' insurance
- holiday pay and sickness pay.

Responsibilities

Both the individual with learning disabilities and social services have specific responsibilities. These are shown in *Box 1* (overleaf). There is usually an independent DP support service that will assist with all of these responsibilities.

Why choose DPs?

As the individual with learning disabilities controls the money, they have more choice, control and flexibility. It means that they can interview and choose their own staff, they can choose the days and times that the person works, and often (depending on the assessment of need) they have more choice over the activities that they do with that person.

Box 1: Respective responsibilities when taking up DPs

What are the service user's responsibilities?

- Recruitment of staff
- Advertising
- Employment issues
- Health and safety
- Completing paperwork for the local authority

What are the responsibilities of social services?

- Assessment of needs
- Identifying risks during assessment process
- Review of needs
- Ensuring needs are met if there is a breakdown of the package

For example, it might be difficult to offer a truly personalised service to each and every individual using regular support, as there are simply not enough in-house staff to work one on one with people all the time. Under DPs the service user can employ a worker dedicated only to them, making it more likely that they can pursue the activities they wish.

Why do we think that DPs works for us?

We have found that there are five main reasons why DPs work for us.

1 **DPs are 'direct'.** Money is paid directly from social services into a bank account, which is used to pay the staff that work with Karen. All the money directly benefits Karen, apart from the tax and national insurance costs. Second, the service is also a direct service to Karen – there are no middlemen, no managers and no contracts. The only people involved are the trustees who are voluntary, Penderels Trust (who help administer the scheme) and the support workers.

2 **DPs are flexible.** We, as trustees, and Karen were involved right at the beginning in deciding the amount of support (hours, days and weeks) that Karen would need in order to have the care she needed in her own flat and the help she needed to access shopping, travelling and community facilities. We were also all involved, with Karen, with recruiting and interviewing staff.

3 **DPs are highly individualised.** The fact that Karen needs different hours of support and different types of support each day means that the package of care is tailor-made to suit her needs. Support workers are provided with a specific job description detailing the support Karen needs for particular activities and corresponding staff responsibilities. Karen chooses her staff and is a good judge of people at interviews!

4 DPs are person-centred. All staffing is one-to-one so that whatever Karen wants to do, she has someone to help her.

5 DPs are straightforward to administer. There is very little paperwork as only two records are essential to keep. One is a record of the hours individual staff work – they sign in when they arrive and leave and Karen countersigns. The second is a record of Karen's expenditure.

DPs clearly work well for Karen and her family – but are there any potential difficulties with using them? Some possible barriers are listed in *Box 2*.

Box 2: What might be the barriers to using DPs?

- There can be difficulties in recruiting suitable personal assistants/support workers.
- The paperwork can be cumbersome and confusing.
- The workers can feel isolated and unsupported, as they are not (usually) part of a team.
- Supervision for workers can be difficult to provide, as service users (the employers) may not be in a position to give this.
- Police checks (CRB checks) are not required legally, but are strongly recommended – and it can take some time for the results to arrive.
- Some care managers and professionals find DPs confusing and prefer not to offer them, despite their duty to do so.
- There are some unanswered questions about what to do in cases where someone meets the criteria to have a DP, but might present a risk to their own workers.
- It can be difficult for someone with a learning disability to open a bank account, which is necessary in order for the local authority to deposit the money.

Summary

DPs are cash payments given in lieu of services to meet needs as assessed by social services. They can transform lives and give people with learning disabilities more control over their lives and the support they need to live as they wish. Councils are now required to offer DPs, and stories such as Karen's are now emerging and encouraging others to take up the scheme.

Catherine, Karen's mother, has seen a huge change in Karen's lifestyle since taking up DPs:

Karen's story

Karen now lives in a two-bedroom flat. She has one bedroom and the staff sleep over in the second bedroom.

It all began in May 2003. Karen and I visited several flats, but each had some reason why they were unsuitable until we heard from an estate agent about a property nearby – a very good location for transport for Karen and quite near to us. By February the housing association had purchased it and we had paid them a quarter share. They consulted Karen about colour of paintwork and height and style of kitchen units and by May Karen was able to move in.

Meanwhile, the DPs were negotiated with help from Penderels Trust and various discussions took place with social services in order to reach an agreement on cost. In order to keep costs down, various concessions were made on both sides. We agreed that Karen would spend every Sunday with us, provided that we could have ten Sundays a year when her staff supported her instead. We also agreed that Karen would spend around seven weeks of the year with us – Christmas, Easter, summer and odd days throughout the year. We applied for housing benefit to pay Karen's rent.

Karen already had a support worker who was employed by an agency but gave notice to be Karen's first support worker. Two other workers were recruited with assistance from Penderels Trust and interviewed by Karen, her advocate, someone from Penderels Trust and I.

In the last two and a half years Karen has had only seven staff – four at present and a rota of three when she first started. One has been with her the whole time and the others have all stayed at least nine months, a very good turnover. We draw up a monthly rota for staff, which is flexible but is mostly the same from week to week as certain staff prefer to work at certain times and on certain days. This takes into account college term times and other variables.

I have been to one session run by Penderels Trust on employment law and at that session all the people receiving DPs for themselves or their relatives agreed how much better it was for them than using agency staff.

Karen's DPs are administered by my husband, my brother and I. Karen chose this arrangement.

'She has complete choice (with help) over what she eats, how and when she does her household tasks and how she spends her leisure time. Karen lives a "normal" life, in that she is in an ordinary flat in an ordinary block of flats, and not a housing unit especially for people with a learning disability. She does not have to live with three or five other people who also have a learning disability and who did not choose to live together. Karen now has a great deal more independence, which, apart from giving her more choice, also increases her self-confidence and also gives her much more power over how she lives her life day to day.'

For more information about self-directed support, go to in Control:
www.in-control.org.uk/home.php

Further reading

Beadle-Brown J (2002) Direct payments for people with severe learning disabilities: a service case study and implications for policy. *Tizard Learning Disability Review* **7** (4) 8–15.

Reference

Department of Health (2004) *Direct Choices: What councils need to make direct payments happen for people with learning disabilities.* London: Department of Health.

Chapter 16

It's my choice

Understanding and promoting advocacy and decision-making

Key words
choice, advocacy, self-advocacy, peer advocacy

Choice

Lloyd Page, *Vice Chair of Inclusion Europe*, writes:

> 'Really very few people are so disabled that they can't make any choices, if they are given the opportunity.

> 'Choice is important to us; it may be a nuisance having to make our minds up, but it is a great deal better than having our minds made up by someone else… or other people pretending that we don't have a mind that we could make up.'
> (Foundation for People with Learning Disabilities, 2000)

Background

The right of people with learning disabilities to make choices has now been recognised by the government. One of the objectives of the white paper, Valuing People (Department of Health, 2001) is:

> 'to enable people with learning disabilities to have as much choice and control as possible over their lives through advocacy and a person-centred approach to planning the services and support they need.'

Some years ago such a statement would have been unimaginable. People with learning disabilities were routinely denied choice. For those in long-stay hospitals, the choice about where they would live, what they would do each day, whom they would associate with and what they would wear and eat was decided for them.

Those living with families might have more choice but, nonetheless, many decisions would be made by other family members and opportunities would be restricted by the way services were organised. For example, it would be assumed that on leaving school the young person would go to an adult training centre or day centre.

For over a quarter of a century, the idea that people with learning disabilities should be empowered and enabled to take control of their lives has gradually gained ground. This has been brought about by various things.

- **The normalisation movement**, which originated in Scandinavia and the USA in the 1960s and early 1970s. This recognised the harm done to people living in large institutions and demanded that the lives of people with learning disabilities should be as close to normal living conditions as possible.
- **The civil rights movement**, which challenged oppression experienced by many minority groups, including people with learning disabilities, and sought to remove barriers to playing a full part in society.
- **The development of a social model of disability** (rather than a medical model), which emphasised the importance of removing these barriers to enable disabled people to be part of their communities.
- The growth of a self-advocacy movement.
- **Society** as a whole has placed more emphasis on individual choice.
- John O'Brien formulated the **five service accomplishments**: community presence; choice; competence; respect; and participation, which many agencies acknowledged as the values underpinning their services (O'Brien & Tyne, 1981).

Problems with making choice a reality

It takes a long time to change attitudes and gain acceptance for the idea that people with learning disabilities can and should make choices. Although many agencies paid lip service to O'Brien's five principles, the reality was often that choice was limited, particularly if someone had a severe learning disability.

If there is to be choice, then opportunities need to be provided so that people can experience a range of options. Often people have led very restricted lives and need to be introduced gradually to choices.

'One way in which people learn about their own preferences and abilities is by trying out new experiences.' (Mental Health Foundation, 1996)

- People need to be listened to and their choices respected. This demands time for staff and others to hear what people are saying and flexibility in services to accommodate choice and change.
- If people with learning disabilities use few or no words, then those close to them need to establish a way of communicating together, so that their preferences can be established.
- Some people will need support in making choices and in this respect the advocacy movement is very important.
- Care staff have a crucial role to play in enabling those they support to make choices.

The development of the advocacy movement

With the growing emphasis on rights and inclusion, an advocacy movement developed. The first group organised by people with learning disabilities in the USA was formed in Oregon in 1973 and was called People First. Similar groups were formed in Scandinavia in the early 1970s.

The different kinds of advocacy

There are two main types of advocacy:

- **self-advocacy**, defined as people speaking up for themselves
- **citizen advocacy**, where citizen advocates (ie. volunteers) create a relationship with a person with learning disabilities, seeking to understand and represent their views.

Self-advocacy

In self-advocacy groups, members give each other mutual support and usually have a facilitator to assist them. In addition to speaking up for themselves individually, the range of activities in which members have been involved have included:

- consciousness-raising sessions
- encouraging members to adopt new roles, such as involvement in staff selection
- campaigns to get rid of old terminology

- direct action, such as improving transport facilities for disabled people
- campaigns to change policy and the law
- promoting direct payments
- involvement in service planning
- involvement in research
- organising national and international conferences
- addressing the United Nations (Emerson *et al*, 2000).

Citizen advocacy

'Citizen advocacy is needed for people with severe learning disabilities because their access to services and other facilities may depend on their having someone to speak up on their behalf… citizen advocates are needed because others involved in the lives of people with learning disabilities are likely to have pressures on them which prevent them from being independent and objective.' (Brooke & Harris, 2000)

In citizen advocacy, the focus is likely to be on the needs and wishes of the individual. There is a challenge still to be addressed in how to hear the voice of those with the most severe disabilities in the planning of services.

Other forms of advocacy include:
- peer advocacy
- short-term or crisis advocacy
- children's and youth advocacy.

Peer advocacy, where people with learning disabilities speak up on behalf of people with more severe learning disabilities, if it were to expand, might enable people's views to be more clearly heard in the planning of services as well as providing a valuable voice for individuals.

Short-term or crisis advocacy is needed when someone has a particularly pressing issue such as a place to live or a serious medical problem. If the person has a severe disability it is important that they know the person already, to be sure they were conveying their wishes.

Children's and youth advocacy has not been widely developed, but could have an important role to play in raising the consciousness of young people to their rights and opportunities.

Problems in the development of the advocacy movement

Often, the development of the movement in England has been hampered by inadequate and/or time-limited funding. Some groups are dependent on bodies such as charitable trusts. Others receive grants from local authorities or health trusts. This, in turn, can create problems. It is important that groups are independent of services. Other issues to bear in mind are listed below.

- It is often hard to recruit and retain sufficient volunteers.
- Sections 1 and 2 of the Disabled Persons Act 1986 would have provided everyone with the right to an advocate and required the development of an independent advocacy service by every authority, but they have never been implemented.
- The movement has remained fragmentary and vulnerable.
- Advocates have not always been recognised.

'The (Pathways to Citizen Advocacy) project heard a number of accounts where citizen advocates were denied access to residential homes or day centres, or refused information relating to major concerns about their partner. There were also instances of advocates being ignored by service commissioners or providers – or even told outright that as advocates they had no standing.' (Foundation for People with Learning Disabilities, 2000)

The relationship of the advocate with others

It is clear that the wishes of the self-advocate should be paramount. For people with learning disabilities in an advocacy partnership, there will be other people who are also close to them, such as the keyworker, care staff, family and friends. There will need to be respect for one another and sensitivity to the different roles that people play in the life of the person with learning disabilities, to ensure that their voice is truly heard.

Challenges for the future

A key challenge for services in England and Wales was set out in Valuing People:

'to have a range of independent advocacy services in each area so that people with learning disabilities can choose the one which best meets their needs'.

It set aside £1.3 million per year for each of the three years, 2001–2004. This money was intended to:

- establish a National Citizen Advocacy Network led by a consortium of leading voluntary organisations. It will be charged with distributing funds to local groups in an equitable and open manner. The funding is not to be used to replace existing funding sources for citizen advocacy. The British Institute of Learning Disabilities (BILD) has been commissioned by the Department of Health to play the leading role
- increase funding for local self-advocacy groups and strengthen the national infrastructure for self-advocacy. Values into Action has been asked and has agreed to work with self-advocacy groups to achieve this.

The money set aside to date will only go some way to the fulfilment of the government's long-term aim.

A second challenge concerns tensions between different groups. Some follow the principles of Wolfensberger (1983) and believe in complete independence, insisting that advocates should receive no rewards in terms of remuneration and academic credits. Others are more pragmatic, perhaps paying some advocates or operating within charitable organisations providing a contracted-out service. These tensions are likely to continue to exist, but it will be important to ensure that the vision of the advocacy movement is not lost.

Conclusion

When Barb Goode addressed the General Assembly of the United Nations in 1992, she said:

'Our voice may be a new one to many of you but you should better get used to hearing it.

Many of us still have to learn how to speak up.

Many of you still have to learn how to listen to us and how to understand us.

We demand that you give us the right to make choices and decisions regarding our own lives.

We are tired of people telling us what to do, what they want. Instead, let us work together as a team.'

That is the ongoing task.

Further reading

Foundation for People with Learning Disabilities (2000) *Choice Discovered. A video and training materials*. London: Mental Health Foundation.

References

Brooke J and Harris J (2000) *Pathways to Citizen Advocacy*. Kidderminster: BILD.

Department of Health (2001) *Valuing People: A new strategy for learning disability for the 21st century*. London: The Stationery Office.

Emerson E, Hatton C, Felce D and Murphy G (2000) *Learning Disabilities: The fundamental facts*. London: Mental Health Foundation.

Foundation for People with Learning Disabilities (2000) *Everyday Lives, Everyday Choices for People with Learning Disabilities and High Support Needs*. London: Mental Health Foundation.

Goode B (1992) Address to the UN General Assembly. *ILSMH News* **14** Brussels, ILSMH (now Inclusion International). Quoted in: L Ward (Ed) (1998) *Innovations in Advocacy and Empowerment*. Chorley: Lisieux Hall Publications.

Mental Health Foundation (1996) *Building Expectations: Opportunities and services for people with a learning disability*. London: Mental Health Foundation.

O'Brien J and Tyne A (1981) *The Principle of Normalisation: A foundation for effective services*. London: Campaign for Mentally Handicapped People: Community and Mental Handicap Educational and Research Association.

Wolfensberger W (1983) *Reflections on the Status of Citizen Advocacy*. Toronto: National Institute of Mental Retardation.

Michelle McCarthy

Chapter 17

Intimate lives

Sexuality and people with learning disabilities

Key words
sexuality, gender, homophobia, heterosexism

In the past, the sexual rights, needs and feelings of people with learning disabilities were ignored or deliberately repressed. But more recently (ie. since the 1970s) the sexuality of people with learning disabilities has been acknowledged. Most services today recognise their role in helping adults with learning disabilities to express their sexuality. However, this is a difficult and delicate task, as sexual matters are not usually freely discussed in our society. Sexual matters are generally considered to be highly personal to the individual. Consequently, addressing sexuality issues can give rise to feelings of embarrassment, fear or shame on the part of both staff and service users.

Defining terms

Table 1 (overleaf) lists some terms you should be familiar with. Note that they are not always used in exactly the same way by everybody, but the definitions given here will provide you with a good starting point for further reading and discussion.

Table 1: Definition of terms

Term	Definition
Sex	The biology of a person, whether they are female or male. Therefore, a sex difference would be that women give birth to children.
Gender	A culturally shaped group of attributes and behaviours assigned to the male or female. Therefore, a gender difference would be that women (rather than men) usually look after children.
Sexuality	The organisation, expression and direction of sexual desire, love, loyalty, passion, affection and intimacy.
Sexual identity	A sense of one's own sexuality.
Sexual orientation	A natural inclination towards a particular sexual identity.
Homophobia	An irrational fear or disgust of lesbians and gay men.
Heterosexism	A belief that heterosexuality is more normal, more natural, more morally right than homosexuality.

Understanding and responding to sexuality issues

The following list provides a framework for understanding and responding to sexuality and each part is explained below:

- acknowledge people's aspirations
- respect people's rights
- help people understand risks
- help people understand their responsibilities.

Acknowledge people's aspirations

Many, though by no means all, people with learning disabilities wish to form intimate adult relationships. These are often expressed in terms of wanting a girl/boyfriend, wanting to be engaged or married or wanting to have children. To what extent these are the actual desires of individuals and how far people are governed by wanting to conform to society's norms and expectations, is as impossible to separate out for people with learning disabilities, as it is for other people. Nevertheless, what we can observe is:

- people's stated desires do not always match their actual behaviour (eg. a man with learning disabilities may say he wants a girlfriend and wants to get married, yet only seeks out other men for sexual partners)
- the aspirations or priorities of families and service providers often do not match what people with learning disabilities want (eg. families and services often see the risks in sexual relationships, whereas people with learning disabilities tend to see the benefits).

The harsh reality of life for many people with learning disabilities is that their aspirations may be not be met, for example they may not achieve a happy and lasting relationship. It is important to remember that many other people do not achieve this either – we have a very high divorce rate and countless other people, regardless of their sexual orientation, do not manage to sustain the kinds of sexual relationships they would ideally like. In a sense, that is just the way life is and little can be done about it. But importantly, many barriers are unnecessarily put in the way of people with learning disabilities and there is much that can and should be done about that.

Respect people's rights

Since sexuality issues have started to be addressed, there has been constant debate about the sexual rights of people with learning disabilities. Most staff in learning disability services tend to say, when asked, that people with learning disabilities should have the same sexual rights as everybody else. This is as it should be (except there are some important legal differences regarding being able to consent to sex), but does not get us very far in determining what those rights might be. The suggested list of rights in *Box 1* (overleaf) would, I think, be accepted by most people.

Help people understand risks

There are certain inherent risks to engaging in sexual behaviours and these are essentially the same for people with learning disabilities as anyone else. Broadly speaking there are three types of risks:

- physical (eg. pregnancy, sexually transmitted infections, damage to sensitive parts of the body)
- emotional or psychological (eg. being upset or rejected by a partner, being abused)
- social (eg. gaining a 'bad' reputation, paying the price for disregarding social norms).

Box 1: A list of sexuality rights

- To be acknowledged as a sexual being and therefore allowed any sexual expression within the law.
- To be free from the prejudices and theories of others (for example, to have a same-sex partner without people assuming it is through lack of choice or information).
- To have privacy for sexual expression.
- To have access to appropriate sex education and support.
- To have access to the means of protection from unwanted pregnancy, sexually transmitted infections and sexual assault.
- To be recognised as a man or woman (not a genderless person).
- To have children?

Note: The last in the list has a question mark against it to reflect the fact that the right to have children is not widely accepted but, in fact, still highly contested for people with learning disabilities.

It is not the role of staff in learning disability services to help service users avoid all risks – this is not possible. However it is appropriate to do the following:

- help people with learning disabilities understand what risks they may face
- help them judge which are worthwhile risks (eg. understanding there are no guarantees of success at the start of a new relationship)
- help them learn what steps to take to avoid serious and unpleasant consequences (eg. of sexual abuse, unwanted pregnancy, HIV/Aids).

Help people understand their responsibilities

Learning disability services have responsibilities to their users. For example, to provide proactive sex education and support, and to provide an environment that is conducive to a responsible and adult attitude to sex (by ensuring privacy and respect). However, people with learning disabilities also have responsibilities when it comes to sexuality. At a minimum level these would include:

- trying to understand the potential consequences of their behaviour
- to ask for help with things they don't understand
- not to abuse or offend others
- to accept and take on board the information and support offered.

Clearly, being able to take responsibility in these ways will be closely related to the level of learning disability a person has and having the capacity to understand and act on their responsibilities.

Sexual health

A broad definition of sexual health would be '*sexual activity which enables a person to keep physically and psychologically well*'. However, in the learning disability field, a much narrower range of concerns have predominated and these have focused on the avoidance of sexually transmitted infections, most notably, HIV (human immunodeficiency virus). Although people with learning disabilities as a 'group' would not appear in any list of those most at risk of HIV, if they engage in high-risk sexual activities, they (like anyone else) clearly can become infected themselves and pass the infection onto others.

Therefore, in recent years, efforts have been made in some learning disability services to:

- educate service users about safer sex
- educate staff about how they might assess and manage HIV risks (see *Chapter 5*).

Reproductive health

People with learning disabilities are as entitled to participate in, and benefit from, health checks and screening programmes, as any other people. They will need clear information and advice about those checks they may be able to do themselves, such as checks for lumps in the breast and testicles and to see medical staff for those checks that need to be done by them, such as looking for signs of cervical and prostate cancer.

When people with learning disabilities are to be taken for health screenings, such as a cervical screening, they need to be thoroughly prepared for what will be involved. Not preparing people adequately can lead to significant distress and consequent lack of co-operation, which could result in the screening having to be abandoned.

The needs of women with learning disabilities regarding the menopause have traditionally been overlooked. However, all women with learning disabilities, who are capable of understanding, should know that they will not continue to have periods for the whole of their lives. Obviously for younger women this information will seem more abstract and less meaningful than for women who are actually approaching the menopause. Allowing for individual variations, women with learning disabilities in their late 40s/early 50s should be prepared for the onset of their menopause. For women with Down's syndrome, who are likely to experience the menopause somewhat earlier than others, this preparation work should take place earlier. Some women will have heard of the terms 'the change' or 'change of life' but not have a clear idea of what this means. The importance of preparing a woman for the bodily changes she may experience is very important, as some of the physical symptoms of the menopause can be alarming and distressing. However, during the preparation, it is important to avoid frightening women about what they might experience.

Services have a duty to see that menopausal women with learning disabilities get the medical care they need, for example, if they are prescribed HRT, this should be regularly reviewed. Alongside this, other 'well woman' checks and breast screenings need to be encouraged during this mid-life phase.

Contraception

Avoiding an unwanted pregnancy is an important part of sex between women and men. However, contraception is usually highly available to women with learning disabilities, but sometimes provided in an insensitive way. They are often given little choice or information about using long-term contraception. Men with learning disabilities are usually not considered to have any responsibilities regarding contraception, because of the general attitude in society that contraception is the responsibility of women.

When contraception is being considered for a woman with learning disabilities, it is essential to explore whether she really needs it. In other words, is she having, or intending to have, vaginal intercourse? Does she have painful periods that may benefit from being put on contraception? These things are important to know, as research and anecdotal evidence suggest that women with learning disabilities are often given contraception when they do not need it. There can be long-term health consequences of this.

Once it has been established that a woman wishes to use some form of contraception, the most appropriate method needs to be chosen. Wherever possible, the woman herself should be fully involved in that decision. The woman's medical history and the practicality of the method need to be taken into account. The injectable contraceptive, Depo-Provera, is disproportionately used with women with learning disabilities, and the same is likely to happen as the newer contraceptive implants become more established. Where doctors are routinely suggesting these for women with learning disabilities, services have a legitimate role in questioning this. While they may be absolutely the right choice for some women, for others there may be better options. Contraception should suit the individual woman, not be given because some methods are more convenient to carers and services.

Sexual abuse

Sexual abuse and exploitation of people with learning disabilities is unfortunately a very common occurrence. A lot of research and practice-based evidence has emerged in recent years, which can leave us in no doubt about this. People with learning disabilities are vulnerable to sexual abuse for many reasons, including:

- being accustomed to being told what to do by others
- lack of education about sex and about abuse
- lack of self-esteem and assertiveness (ie. not realising they have the right not to be abused)
- not being believed when they speak about what has happened
- living in environments where they are exposed to many potential perpetrators (other people with learning disabilities, staff, volunteers, etc)
- not being valued and protected members of society.

Only those people who have severe or profound learning disabilities are legally defined as being unable to consent to sexual relationships. However, there can still be problems with determining consent to sex for some people, even for those with mild and moderate learning disabilities. Consent to sex should only be seen as valid if the person genuinely understands what they are saying yes to and if they have a real option (ie. no adverse consequences) of saying no. This means, in practice, that people need to understand the nature and the consequences of sexual acts, plus not experience any pressure, threats or fear in making their decision.

The law has traditionally not been very responsive to sexual crimes committed against people with learning disabilities. However, the Sexual Offences Act (2003) (the relevant learning disability sections are 30–44) increased the range of sexual offences against people with learning disabilities and also the severity of the sentences, if the accused are found guilty.

Sexuality in the context of race, culture and religion

In recent years there has been a growing recognition of the need to respect the diversity in race, culture and religion of people with learning disabilities. Many learning disability services now try to provide support that is sensitive to the specific needs of clients from minority ethnic backgrounds. Obviously providing sexuality support should be no different. However, this is hard to do as there are tensions and disagreements within and between cultures about various forms of sexual expression.

The kinds of tensions that might arise between people with learning disabilities, their families and services could include the following examples.

- The parents of a Muslim woman with learning disabilities refuse permission for their daughter to attend a mixed personal relationships course.
- The family of a Roman Catholic man with learning disabilities do not want him to be taught about safer sex, as use of condoms is not sanctioned by their religion.
- The parents of an Asian woman with learning disabilities are arranging her marriage, but staff at her day service feel she does not understand what this means.
- A man with learning disabilities from an Orthodox Jewish background is known to have sex with other men, and believes his religion permits this, when in fact it does not.

Staff in learning disability services should take great care before making assumptions about what a particular culture's beliefs and practices about sexuality are. Where possible, this should be discussed with the person with learning disabilities themselves. When this is not possible, or to supplement that information, good practice would be to seek advice from a number of representatives of a certain culture and, if appropriate, from the family.

To avoid potential conflict between individuals, their families and services, it is useful to recognise that all parties have a shared commitment to the well-being of the person with learning disabilities. Since, in practice, most sexuality work with people with learning disabilities prioritises safety issues, this provides a good basis for interventions that should satisfy all concerned. Perceived or real cultural influences should not be accepted as a reason to deny people with learning disabilities the information and skills they need to protect themselves from exploitation and abuse.

Conclusion

People with learning disabilities have a right to support with the sexual part of their lives. Those supporting them need to be aware of the reality of people's lives and circumstances, and tailor their support accordingly. Those who support them should also remember that, although intimate relationships and sexual expression may be problematic for some people with learning disabilities, so they are for many other people too. This is easy to forget when it is always 'their' sexual lives under scrutiny, and not 'ours'.

Further reading

Craft A (1994) *Practice Issues in Sexuality and Learning Disabilities*. London: Routledge.

McCarthy M (1999) *Sexuality and Women with Learning Disabilities*. London: Jessica Kingsley Publishers.

McCarthy M (2002) Going through the menopause: perceptions and experiences of women with intellectual disabilities. *Journal of Intellectual and Developmental Disability* **27** (4) 281–295.

McCarthy M and Thompson D (2007) *Sex and the 3 Rs: Rights, responsibilities and risks (3rd edition)*. Brighton: Pavilion Publishing (Brighton) Ltd.

Malhotra S and Mellan B (1996) Cultural and race issues in sexuality work with people with learning difficulties. *Tizard Learning Disability Review* **1** (4) 7–12.

Chapter 18

Family matters

Working with parents with learning disabilities

Key words
capacity, knowledge, skills and practice, legal context, rights and responsibilities, appropriate support

It is only in more recent years, with changes in the philosophy of services, that people with learning disabilities have had more freedom with regard to their relationships and sexuality. One of the consequences is that the number of people with learning disabilities having children is increasing (Department of Health, 2001). These parents are much more likely than other parents to have their children taken into care (Department of Health, 2001).

Parenting is a very difficult task indeed. As well as having intellectual limitations, parents with learning disabilities frequently experience a large range of difficulties that also make the job of parenting harder, such as poverty, poor housing, social isolation and limited networks of friends and sources of support. However, the difficulties that they experience cannot be accounted for by these social problems alone. It is, of course, very important to consider and respect the 'rights' of people with learning disabilities. However, it is vital that people working with these families remember that the welfare of the child takes absolute priority over everything else. This can lead to staff experiencing tension between their client (the parent) and the child's needs.

How many?

We do not know exactly how many parents with learning disabilities there are in the UK. This is because different services use different definitions of learning disabilities and not all families are known to services. However, it is suggested that there are 250,000 parents with learning disabilities in the UK (McGaw, 1996), although some studies argue that this figure might be lower. Families can often be referred to services at a very late stage in a pregnancy or when significant concerns about their parenting skills have been present for a considerable period of time. Evidence suggests that interventions are less likely to be successful when families are already experiencing high levels of difficulties, are in crisis, or there are very significant concerns about the child. The earlier these families can be identified and supported the better, particularly in terms of parents being willing to accept help (McGaw, 1996).

Removal rates

In the UK it is suggested that between 40–60% of children of parents with learning disabilities are taken into care (Booth & Booth, 2004). It is common that parents hide any difficulties that they are experiencing, out of a very real fear that their child(ren) will be taken away.

Difficulties that children face

Children of parents with a learning disability can certainly be described as vulnerable. They are at more risk of having their development delayed, especially in language and cognitive skills, compared with children from other similar families who do not have a learning disability (Keltner *et al*, 1999). Mothers with learning disabilities are likely to interact less with their children – in ways such as praising good behaviour and repeating a child's noises – than parents without disabilities (Feldman *et al*, 1986). However, it has also been shown that some mothers are able to learn more appropriate interactions and that these improvements were still evident 20 months later (Feldman *et al*, 1993).

Children of parents with learning disabilities are also likely to do less well at school and have greater behaviour problems than other impoverished children whose parents did not have a learning disability (Feldman & Walton-Allen, 1997). It is estimated that at least 60% of parents with learning disabilities will have children who are more able than themselves (McGaw, 1998).

Historically, it has been considered that children of these parents are at greater risk of experiencing abuse. It is rare for mothers with learning disabilities to deliberately abuse their child (McGaw & Newman, 2005). When abuse does occur it is often by a person known to the mother (often partner) who has emotional difficulties or takes part in criminal behaviour (McGaw & Newman, 2005). It appears that children can be at greatest risk of *'unintentional neglect'* (Tymchuk & Andron, 1992) because parents, through a lack of education, often do not know what to do and struggle to know how to improve their parenting.

Mothers that do well

Tymchuk and Andron (1994) report that the features of mothers with learning disabilities who do well with their parenting include adequate reading and comprehension skills (a reading age of approximately nine years – so that people can read labels, instructions etc), an IQ over 60, no emotional difficulties, no medical problems, low stress, adequate self-concept and motivation. They also report external factors that contribute to success, such as having only one child, a younger child, a child without medical or other problems, a partner without emotional disturbance or criminal behaviour, having sufficient supports, not having lived in an institution, having had good role models in their own childhood, having adequately trained professionals, materials that are appropriate to teach skills, continuity of agency involvement and services that are well co-ordinated across agencies (Tymchuk & Andron, 1994). In the past, an individual's IQ has been seen as critical to whether parents can provide adequate parenting. The literature indicates that an individual's IQ does not relate to competent parenting skills unless it falls below 60 (McGaw, 1998).

Supporting parents with learning disabilities

'The best predictor of future parental competency for parents with intellectual disabilities is the quality and frequency of social and practical support available to them on a daily basis.' (McGaw, 1998)

Support for parents with learning disabilities is a major factor in determining whether they are successful in their parenting. These parents are often very isolated and don't have the usual sources of support that are available to many people, such as friends, neighbours and families (McGaw, 1997). In addition, parents with learning disabilities may experience difficulties accessing 'mainstream' parenting resources such as magazines, groups, courses etc, as they are likely to experience difficulty with written information. Such information is also frequently presented in a manner that is too complicated for people with learning disabilities to understand. The way that information is presented and the pace of groups will all need to be modified for this group of parents. The author has run a group about play that is specifically modified for parents with learning disabilities, and one of the overriding themes of the feedback was that this group of parents greatly valued the opportunity to meet other parents who faced similar challenges with parenting to themselves.

The Parent Assessment Manual (PAM) (McGaw *et al*, 1999) is a very useful assessment tool that has been developed specifically for this group of parents. In the assessment there were three key components to a thorough assessment of parenting. This can help identify areas for support and teaching.

Knowledge

This section assesses what a parent knows about a particular area of childcare. Obviously knowledge has to be in place prior to being able to learn and maintain any skills in relation to that task. On occasions, parents may already have skills in the area where their knowledge has been assessed as poor. Without the knowledge of why these skills are necessary, it is unlikely that these skills will be consistently used. Studies have shown that simply giving people knowledge does not mean that this knowledge is put into practice (Bakken *et al*, 1993; Tymchuk & Andron, 1992).

Skills

This section assesses whether people actually have the abilities to carry out the tasks required for parenting. In a review of 20 studies that looked at teaching parents with learning disabilities new skills, Feldman (1994) concluded that parents learn best when they are shown skills (modelling), given the chance to practise and given feedback and praise for success. It is preferable to teach the skills in the environment in which they need to be used ie. at home, or if this is not possible, try and make it as similar to home as possible.

Practice

This section assesses whether people actually carry out the skills as and when they are needed. It is possible that people may have the knowledge and the skills, but don't do what they need to do at the time that the skills are required. For example, parents may know how to make up a bottle but don't do it every time they need to.

When a comprehensive assessment highlights what difficulties there are with parenting (eg. is it someone's knowledge in a particular area that needs to be tackled first?), it is then possible to ensure that interventions are put in place in order to address these.

Services

It is generally known that outcomes for families are better if all the services working with these families work together in a co-ordinated manner. This sounds simple enough but in reality can often be difficult to achieve, as services tend to be organised around specific client groups – such as children or adults with learning disabilities – and interventions focus on that single group only. McConnell *et al* (1997) recommend that services need to be 'family centred' and that as a result both parents' and children's needs are considered. It is often the case that there are a large number of workers supporting a family and it is important to consider whether this is overwhelming to individuals, which can lead to parents being less inclined to accept support.

Families with parents who have learning disabilities tend to require help on a long-term basis throughout the duration of the child's life, although the frequency of that support can vary at different times. It is important that staff working with these families are honest and respectful and have a positive attitude in trying to promote competence. Often professionals working within services have had very little experience or training in working with parents with learning disabilities. Given this, it is vital that they themselves receive training and supervision with this task.

Services for parents with learning disabilities are rather varied across the country. In all but a few areas there are no specialist services for parents who have learning disabilities. As a result there is often a lack of funding for the support services that are required. It can be unclear who should fund such support and as a result families often fall in the gaps between services. In Cornwall, for example, there is a specialist service that was established in 1988. To find out more visit www.cornwall.nhs.uk/specialparentingservices.

Solicitors and court proceedings

A large number of these families have their children removed. This means that they have to go through 'care proceedings', which is a legal process that decides whether children remain in the care of their parents. This is an extremely stressful time for these parents, and families can find it difficult to understand some of the issues and complexities of the court processes. Parents need access to good solicitors who understand learning disabilities. They are also likely to need help and support throughout the court process.

Conclusions

Children of parents with learning disabilities are at risk of a significant number of difficulties, such as developmental delay, behaviour problems etc. However, there is evidence that these parents can learn new skills and knowledge when it is presented and taught in appropriate ways. These families are likely to require help and support on a long-term basis. In order to adequately support such families they require comprehensive multi-agency assessments that are aimed at promoting the competencies of these parents. It is important that staff working with families refer on to specialist services in order to ensure that such assessments and interventions are provided.

Working with parents with learning disabilities can be an emotionally challenging experience. At times it challenges one's own beliefs and values, and at times it can be distressing, particularly when families are not able to stay together. As a result of this it is important to ensure that workers receive good supervision and support as they take on this role.

Further reading

There are some very helpful resources available that can help parents with learning disabilities to learn skills so that their parenting is 'good enough'. Some of those available are listed below.

CHANGE (2004) *You and Your Baby 0–1 Year Picture Bank CD-rom*. Available from: www.changepeople.co.uk.

Feldman M (1986) Research on parenting by mentally retarded persons. *Psychiatric Clinics of North America* **9** (4) 777–796.

McGaw S and Newman T (2005) *What Works for Parents with Learning Disabilities?* Ilford, Essex: Barnardo's.

McGaw S and Smith K (1998) *Parenting Skill Cards Set 2: Children need healthy food*. Kidderminster: BILD.

McGaw S and Tornabene A (2000) *Parenting Skill Cards Set 3: Children need to be clean, healthy and warm*. Kidderminster: BILD.

McGaw S and Tornabene A (2000) *Parenting Skill Cards Set 5: What is love?* Kidderminster: BILD.

McGaw S and Valentine D (2002) *Parenting Skill Cards Set 4: Children need to be safe*. Kidderminster: BILD.

Tarleton B, Ward L and Howarth J (2006) *Finding the Right Support: A review of issues and positive practice to support parents with learning difficulties and their children*. London: The Baring Foundation.

References

Bakken J, Miltenberger RG and Schauss S (1993) Teaching parents with mental retardation: knowledge versus skills. *American Journal on Mental Retardation* **97** (4) 405–417.

Booth T and Booth W (2004) A family at risk: multiple perspectives on parenting and child protection. *British Journal of Learning Disabilities* **32** (1) 9–16.

Department of Health (2001) *Valuing People: A new strategy for learning disability for the 21st century*. London: The Stationery Office.

Feldman M (1994) Parenting education for parents with intellectual disabilities: a review of outcome studies. *Research in Developmental Disabilities* **15** (4) 299–332.

Feldman M, Sparks B and Case L (1993) Effectiveness of home-based early intervention on the language development of children of mothers with mental retardation. *Research in Developmental Disabilities* **14** (5) 387–408.

Feldman M, Towns F, Betel J, Case L, Rincover A and Rubino CA (1986) Parent education project II. Increasing stimulating interactions of developmentally handicapped mothers. *Journal of Applied Behavior Analysis* **19** (1) 23–37.

Feldman M and Walton-Allen N (1997) Effects of maternal mental retardation and poverty on intellectual, academic and behavioural status of school age children. *American Journal of Mental Retardation* **101** (4) 354–364.

Keltner B, Wise L and Taylor G (1999) Mothers with intellectual limitations and their two year old children's developmental outcomes. *Journal of Intellectual and Developmental Disabilities* **24** (1) 45–57.

McConnell D, Llewelyn G and Bye R (1997) Providing services for parents with intellectual disability – parent needs and service constraints. *Journal of Intellectual and Developmental Disability* **22** (1) 5–17.

McGaw S (1996) Services for parents with learning disabilities. *Tizard Learning Disability Review* **1** (1) 21–28.

McGaw S (1997) Practical support for parents with learning disabilities. In: J O'Hara and A Sperlinger (Eds) (1997) *Adults with Learning Disabilities*. Chichester: Wiley.

McGaw S (1998) Working with parents who happen to have intellectual disabilities. In: E Emerson, C Hatton, J Bromley and A Caine (Eds) (1998) *Clinical Psychology and People with Intellectual Disabilities*. Chichester: Wiley.

McGaw S, Beckley K, Connolly N and Ball K (1999) *Parenting Assessment Manual*. Truro: Trecare NHS Trust.

McGaw S and Newman T (2005) *What Works for Parents with Learning Disabilities?* Ilford, Essex: Barnardo's.

Tymchuk AJ and Andron L (1992) Project parenting: child interactional training with mothers who are mentally handicapped. *Mental Handicap Research* **5** (1).

Tymchuk AJ and Andron L (1994) Rationale, approaches, results and resource implications of programmes to enhance parenting skills of people with learning disabilities. In: A Craft *Practice Issues in Sexuality and Learning Disabilities*. Routledge: London.

Chapter 19

Issues across the lifepath
Managing change, transition and loss

Key words
control, predictability, involvement, loss

This chapter addresses some of the ways that people with learning disabilities can be supported around times of transition and loss. Major changes, such as a move, bereavement or the start or ending of a significant relationship, can be emotionally taxing for anyone. For people who are marginalised, or who struggle with making sense of their world because of limited communication skills or additional disabilities, managing such major changes can be even more difficult. The chapter makes reference to some practical ways in which it is possible to reduce the confusion and emotional turmoil that people with learning disabilities may experience at times of loss and transition.

Saying goodbye, saying hello
Frequent changes can be a feature in the lives of many people with learning disabilities, not least when establishing and ending relationships with the staff who support them in day and residential settings. As many people with learning disabilities are dependent on carers to help meet their physical, social and emotional needs, the relationship between staff and service users can become very important. However, with a high turnover of staff, it is not uncommon for people with learning disabilities to regularly experience separation and loss when keyworkers with whom they have established a relationship move away. Mattison and Pistrang (2000) have written a thought-

provoking and engaging account of a series of interviews with keyworkers and people with learning disabilities in residential homes about the experience of keyworkers leaving. They found that these separations were often far more emotionally significant for people with learning disabilities than many of the staff had imagined. Mattison and Pistrang comment:

'Care staff may devalue their own role in clients' lives, perhaps partly because the staff themselves are not valued within the service where they work. For keyworkers who do recognise the importance of their role, it can be hard to tolerate the responsibility and guilt of leaving. This in turn may make it difficult to acknowledge or attend to the client's feelings of loss.'

All the residents whom Mattison and Pistrang interviewed about endings said that they much preferred to be given plenty of notice about the departure of their keyworker so that they could better prepare themselves. Their preference echoes conclusions made in other studies that have shown that helping people with learning disabilities to anticipate and plan for endings can significantly reduce the impact of loss (Siebold, 1991).

Anticipating and planning endings may take many forms and will, to some degree, be determined by the individual's level of functioning. However, an important part of managing change involves finding accessible and meaningful ways of informing people with learning disabilities about events that affect them, such as the departure of significant people in their lives. This is a task that should not just be left to the individual workers who are leaving but also requires the active involvement and contributions of those who remain. Staff who remain may need to reinforce a message that the person has left and may find themselves having important conversations with the person with learning disabilities about the staff member after they've gone.

Many of us who have worked closely with people with learning disabilities will have found ourselves, at the point of saying goodbye, making vague promises about keeping in touch, as a way of easing the pain of leaving. Studies and experience show that, while well intentioned, this is generally unhelpful to the person leaving, the person left behind and to the staff who come after.

The process of saying goodbye is, of course, about more than the sadness that endings often evoke. It can also involve reviewing memories of times spent together and things that have been accomplished. The use of photos, drawings, objects, sensory experiences and words may all facilitate this task. Additionally, the marking of endings can act as the bridge to the future, to new opportunities and new relationships. New keyworkers may bring enriching new relationships, new understandings and may act as facilitators of new developments.

Attending to how new people are received and welcomed into services is just as important as thinking about endings. Preparation for the arrival of a new person in a service can significantly shape the success or failure of the experience for all concerned. This preparation is equally important, whether the 'new' person is a tenant with learning disabilities, or a member of staff joining the support team. An example in the section on transitions below provides details about some of the preparations for a resident's move to a new home.

Transitions

Change is both an important and inevitable part of growth and development. Whether changes are positive (eg. a job promotion, a move to better accommodation) or negative (eg. the sudden end of a relationship, the diagnosis of an illness), they trigger reactions and require a period of adjustment. Studies of the effect of transitions have shown that transitions are most stressful if they are *unpredictable* (eg. the sudden closure of a residential home), *involuntary* (eg. the relocation of one's place of work), *unfamiliar* (eg. moving to a setting where different rules apply or a different language is spoken), and if they are of *high intensity and frequency* (Hopson, 1981). By contrast, research into successful outcomes of transition has shown that, among other things, they depend on:

- involvement of the people affected
- predictability of the event (even if potentially stressful)
- whether the person has control over the duration of the transition
- the availability of social support (see Kobasa *et al*, 1982).

People with learning disabilities are often subject to many changes and transitions over which they have little or no control, choice or involvement. Research has shown that where people are not involved or consulted about major moves and transitions, they fare much worse psychologically when compared with groups of people who have been involved in meaningful ways, who have received relevant and accessible information and where careful planning has taken place (see, for example Collins, 1994).

Moving to a new home is often rated as one of the most stressful events in many stress indexes, even if the move may eventually lead to many positive changes. Overleaf is an example of some of the ways that Sonia was supported to move to a new home in another part of the country.

Case example: Sonia

Sonia, who had a diagnosis of autism and a severe learning disability, needed to move on when the home in which she was living was closing down. The staff who had worked with Sonia over many years knew that she struggled with understanding references to things that might happen in the future, and that she became anxious when things were uncertain and vague. In Sonia's case they felt that she would manage a relatively short transition period best and that they would support her to make sense of what was happening by drawing on her interest in looking at photographs. Once they had received a firm guarantee that Sonia's new home was ready for her, a date was set for her move and the work of helping Sonia to understand what was happening began. The staff team's insistence on having absolute assurance of the moving date was based on their experience of managing all the additional confusion and distress that may arise when delays occur, such as building works over-running or other residents not moving out.

With the moving date established, staff at Sonia's old and new homes could engage in supporting her move. First, Sonia went on a visit with members of staff to her new home. Sonia indicated that she liked her new environment with its safe open spaces, and many photos were taken of Sonia in her new home. Returning home, these photographs were developed and served as an aid for staff to start talking with Sonia about the move. Staff from Sonia's new home worked alongside her old staff team for several shifts in order to learn about some of the more subtle ways of supporting her that it was not always easy to capture in written notes and reports. During Sonia's last week in her old home, a very large calendar with the numbers one to seven was displayed on the wall in her home. Next to the last number in the calendar, a photo of Sonia outside her new home appeared. Pictures were also stuck beside some of the other numbers in the 'count-down calendar'. There were pictures that helped Sonia to understand that: three days before her move she would be going to a local restaurant where she had enjoyed many meals and been made to feel welcome by the owners; two days before she moved there would be a leaving party for her; on the day before she moved, pictures of bags and suitcases indicated that she would be packing her things with her keyworker etc. At the end of every day Sonia and a member of staff used a big red pen to cross out one of the days to signal the progressive countdown.

Sonia also had a large collection of photos that she took with her to her new home. The staff had remembered to date the photos and to write on the back who was in the picture and their relationship to Sonia. The staff were mindful that without such details, people who worked with Sonia in years to come would not be able to talk to her about all the people and places that had been important to her.

Bereavement

A few weeks before the start of a group for people with learning disabilities who had lost a parent, I received a short letter from Paul's main carer:

'I don't want Paul to attend your meetings. He doesn't understand death and never will. It is a year since his Dad died and he has accepted that he isn't coming home anymore. He isn't at all upset and is his happy self. My doctor agrees with me to leave things as they are.'

In a few lines Paul's carer succinctly expresses many of the views and beliefs that have informed responses to people with learning disabilities when they lose a significant person in their life. Historically, it has often been assumed that people with learning disabilities are unable to develop strong attachments and close relationships that are likely to result in feelings of personal loss, and that they therefore do not experience grief (Oswin, 1991; Mattison & Pistrang, 2000). Some of the results of these beliefs and assumptions are listed below.

1 **To overlook grief reactions, or to mislabel them as challenging behaviour** (Emerson, 1977). Hollins and Esterhuyzen (1997) followed 50 people with learning disabilities who had lost a parent and compared them with another group of 50 learning disabled people who had not been bereaved. They found that there was a much higher rate of behavioural and emotional difficulties in the bereaved group compared with the non-bereaved group. In the case of Paul, for instance, while he might have been his happy self at home, the situation at the day centre was very different. There he was tearful and had become very attached to his male keyworker whom he rarely let out of his sight.

2 **To neglect giving clear explanations or to use confusing euphemisms to refer to death**. This was illustrated in Paul's case where his father's death was referred to as *'him not coming home anymore'*.

3 **To rush people with learning disability into institutional care, with little or no explanation, when a main carer dies**. This intervention often removes them from all that is familiar and that gives meaning to their experience (Oswin, 1991).

4 **To exclude people from the social responses and rituals associated with death**. Hollins and Esterhuyzen's research showed that only about half of the bereaved people had been involved in any of the social responses associated with death, such as a funeral.

Studies have indicated that it is indeed possible for people with learning disabilities to understand death and loss (McEvoy, 1989) and that it is important not to assume that a person does not feel any grief because he or she cannot verbally express it (Oswin, 1991). For example, Paul, who had very limited speech, was able to communicate his distress and confusion through his behaviour at the day centre where he demonstrated his fear that another important male figure in his life, his keyworker, might disappear.

As is the case among people *without* learning disabilities, reactions can vary widely and depend on many factors. These might include:

- the nature of the relationship with the person who has died
- the circumstances of death (sudden or unexpected)
- the history of previous losses and how these were resolved.

Sometimes reactions may be delayed or a current loss may evoke previous ones.

There are many ways of supporting people who are experiencing, or have experienced, a loss and there will be many factors that will influence what is and is not appropriate in particular circumstances. Below is a list with some ideas and suggestions, and many others could be added. It is important to remember that each person with learning disability is an individual and will grieve as an individual, although cultural belief systems within which they live and have grown up are likely to play an important part in shaping the way that grief is manifested and expressed.

Working with people before a death

The following are some areas to consider when the death of someone close to an individual with learning disabilities is expected and may also be incorporated into working practices in day centres and residential homes. Being proactive in thinking about and planning for death can reduce the impact of loss (Siebold, 1991) and facilitate the way that grief is processed.

- Create opportunities to talk and check the person's understanding about what is happening.
- Use clear and unambiguous language.
- Have death and dying on the agenda. Use opportune moments, for example death of characters in soaps on television or stories of people or pets who have died, as reference points.
- Get a sense of the person's bereavement history (family members, friends who have died). How were they involved, how did they react?
- Where appropriate, discuss the person's own thoughts about death and acknowledge any anxieties they may have.

- Familiarise people with the idea of funerals, cremations or other ceremonies using visits or resource booklets.

Working with people following a death

- Be open about the death (circumstances and causes).
- Avoid confusing euphemisms ('not coming home anymore', 'gone to sleep' etc).
- Talk about the person who has died and explore memories.
- Many media such as photographs, drawings, life story books, mementos, booklets (eg. Hollins & Sireling, 1989) can be used to facilitate discussions (see ***Further reading***, below).
- Encourage attendance at funerals, memorials and culturally appropriate rituals etc, and, where appropriate, seek to involve the person in meaningful ways (eg. sharing memories about the person who has died).
- Be aware that bereavement reactions may be delayed, or may be triggered by other losses (eg. the departure of a keyworker or moving house).
- Ongoing support is important – be aware of anniversaries and special festivals (eg. Christmas, birthdays or other festivals).

Resources

The past 10 to 15 years have seen the publication of an increasing range of resources about death and bereavement that can be used to facilitate conversations with people with learning disabilities who have experienced a loss. Many of these resources are in the form of colourful booklets, flashcards and videos and can be used with people with few verbal skills. Easily accessible books have also been written for carers and staff groups.

Further reading

Cathcart F (1994) *Understanding Death and Dying*. A series of three booklets for the client, relative and professional carer. Available from BILD.

Cooley J and McGauran F (2001) *Talking Together about Death*. Chesterfield: Winslow Press.

Hollins S and Sireling L (1989) *When Dad Died* and *When Mum Died*. Books without Words series. London: Royal College of Psychiatrists.

Watchman K (2001) *Let's Talk About Death: A booklet about death and funerals for adults who have a learning disability*. Edinburgh: Down's Syndrome Scotland.

References

Collins J (1994) *Still to be Settled: Strategies for the resettlement of people from mental handicap hospitals.* London: Values into Action.

Emerson P (1977) Covert grief reaction in mentally retarded clients. *Mental Retardation* **15** (6) 46–47.

Hollins S and Esterhuyzen (1997) Bereavement and grief in adults with learning disabilities. *British Journal of Psychiatry* **170** (6) 497–501.

Hollins S and Sireling L (1989) *When Dad Died* and *When Mum Died.* Books without Words series. London: Royal College of Psychiatrists.

Hopson B (1981) Transition: Understanding and managing personal change. In: Herbert M (Ed) *Psychology for Social Workers.* London: Macmillan.

Kobasa SC, Madd SR and Kahn S (1982) Hardness and health: a prospective study. *Journal of Personality and Social Psychology* **42** (1) 168–177.

Mattison V and Pistrang N (2000) *Saying Goodbye: When keyworker relationships end.* London: Free Association Books.

McEvoy J (1989) Investigating the concept of death in adults who are mentally handicapped. *The British Journal of Mental Subnormality* **35** 115–121.

Oswin M (1991) *Am I Allowed to Cry? A study of bereavement amongst people with learning difficulties.* London: Human Horizon Series.

Siebold C (1991) Termination: when the therapist leaves. *Clinical Social Work Journal* **19** (2) 191–204.

Chapter 20

Not as young as we used to be

Supporting older people with learning disabilities

Key words

choice, community, diversity, experience, independence, longevity, quality in ageing

The general population in Britain is ageing. It is an issue that has raised much debate, especially with regard to what this increase in the number of older people implies for those with responsibility for providing health and social care. This debate has now crossed over into the field of learning disability. It is recognised that people with learning disabilities are also living longer, many of the present generation reaching ages over 60, and yet there is little consensus in terms of the 'right' kind of service to offer this emerging group of people.

This chapter provides an outline of what is known about older people with learning disabilities, and suggests an agenda for those providing services. It makes reference to both the appropriateness of services for people with learning disabilities and services for older people, in relation to those who are now growing older within the current learning disability service provision. It looks at the importance of training, specifically in the effects and impacts of the ageing process, and finally it highlights some of the key issues for good practice.

What do we know about older people with learning disabilities?

With this newly emerging client group it is fair to say that we know very little. It has been a commonly held belief that people with learning disabilities do not grow old, either in body or in mind, and it seems that services have been unprepared for this inevitability. As with the general population, advances in medical technology have led to improved longevity, and specific advances in perinatal care have led to children with profound and multiple disabilities surviving well beyond the first year of life.

- In the US, it is predicted that 40% of people with learning disabilities will live to the age of 60 and that 12% will live to be over 65.
- In Britain, it was estimated (1991) that 47% of people with learning disabilities were aged over 45 and 17% were over 65. The estimated prevalence rate of over 60s per 1,000 of the British population is between 0.4% and 0.5%.
- It is expected that mortality rates for people with learning disabilities will soon approach those of the general population, taking into account that people with Down's syndrome have a lower life expectancy than other people with learning disabilities.
- As with the general population, it is expected that women, specifically those with mild learning disabilities living in the community, will have the longest life expectancy.
- As yet, there are no conclusive figures regarding the expected prevalence of older people with learning disabilities from minority ethnic communities. However, studies already indicate that the prevalence of learning disabilities among black and ethnic minority children is higher than among white children (in Baxter *et al*, 1990 p28). There is no reason to assume that life expectancy among minority ethnic communities will be any lower than that of the white population.

Ageing family carers

A large number of people with learning disabilities currently live with their parents or carers, and it is increasingly acknowledged that they are outliving them. In addition, older people with learning disabilities were among the last to leave the large institutions. The adaptation – and indeed the acceptance of possessing the ability to adapt to community living, after so many years of institutional or home care and at a greater age – must pose as yet unidentified difficulties for some individuals. The potential of older people with learning disabilities has been greatly underestimated and this has led to marginalisation, limited choices and care options.

How appropriate is current service provision as people grow older?

As with any other group of people in society, we cannot talk about older people with learning disabilities as if they all share the same traits and characteristics, whether those characteristics are associated with learning disability or with older age. The diversity and unique personhood of individuals continues throughout the lifespan, and the heterogeneity of the learning disabled population suggests that a range of services and responses is required to serve the needs of the older people among them. Little is known about the physical, psychological, emotional and social processes of ageing among people with learning disabilities, and as yet the consequences of old age for people with learning disabilities, their families, carers and service providers are unknown.

In recognition of the size of the ageing general population, there has been a move towards encouraging preparation for self-sufficiency in older age. This includes the provision of personal pensions and medical plans, financial savings and purchase of property to cover the cost of residential or nursing home care in later life. The range and spectrum of services available for older people is gradually increasing. It is no longer assumed that older people are simply 'put out to grass in old people's homes', but can be offered home care in the community and minimum or extra-care sheltered housing in addition to the more traditional residential services or long-stay hospital wards. It is also beginning to be recognised that older people have specific needs related to the maintenance of personhood, inclusion, purpose, companionship and the psychological and physical changes associated with ageing. Older people with learning disabilities will have had little opportunity to provide for their old age. For many, state benefits will have been their only income, and the purchase of property well beyond their means. In an increasingly materialistic society this can only limit the choice of future service options available for them within current older person's provision, and this evokes the question of whether a comprehensive range of specialist services should be developed.

Services are fragmented into different specialisms. Service assumptions for older people can often be restricting and disempowering, but service philosophy for people with learning disabilities advocates integration. How advantageous will continued integration be if staff and existing clients of available services for older people have no awareness or understanding of the specific needs of people with learning disabilities? Just as this premise applies to older person's services, it can also apply to services for people with learning disabilities. How appropriate are the principles of 'normalisation' and the attainment of the 'five service accomplishments' (eg. O'Brien & Tyne, 1981) when a traditionally perceived 'normal' and 'valued' lifestyle may not include a desire to be actively integrated into society? After all, many older people prefer to retire quietly into a familiar environment where the emphasis is on being cared for, not being supported to independence.

Applying service principles to older people with learning disabilities has inherent difficulties according to Wolfensberger (1985), and unless there is policy recognition of the particular problems facing older people with learning disabilities, there is a danger of 'double jeopardy'. They are likely to be poorly served by sets of services – those for older people and those for people with learning disabilities.

The providers' agenda: policy recognition and service development

In a key study of community care plans, Robertson *et al* (1996) found that only 33% mentioned older people with learning disabilities. Even though service managers were acutely aware of the need for policy and service development, few areas had worked towards this, and different areas were responding differently to both actual and potential demand. There was evidence that older people with learning disabilities were beginning to be recognised as a specific client group, but the task of providing services for them is difficult.

Service planners and providers need to balance two objectives and provide an accessible range of services that respond to:

- the diverse, age-related needs and difficulties faced by older people with learning disabilities
- the psychological, physical, emotional and social needs associated with the ageing process.

There is a need to maintain autonomy and the potential for making choices, to sustain close personal relationships and enable full use of leisure time for the individual with learning disabilities. There is also a need to see the older person in the context of their whole-life experience and unique personhood. The challenge, therefore, is to respect autonomy, diversity and individuality, while providing additional support where needed with respect to the process of growing older.

Policies for people with learning disabilities have failed to consider the dimension of ageing, even though studies have long recognised the high incidence of disability in older age. Compared with the general population, older people with learning disabilities have a higher prevalence of psychological and physical disorders, and it is also to be assumed that they will not be immune to the illnesses, mental and physical decline associated with the ageing process. Indeed, it is generally accepted that people with Down's syndrome have a higher possibility of Alzheimer's-related dementia.

Great diversity in terms of provision models has led to little consensus in terms of the 'right' kind of service to offer older people with learning disabilities. In planning appropriate services it is vital to take into account:

- the size of the local population
- *actual* as well as *perceived* need
- physical and mental healthcare needs, specifically in relation to dementia
- social care needs, and age-associated community links
- accessible housing, providing security within a familiar and adaptable environment
- inter-agency collaboration and accessibility to community health and social services
- a spectrum of services ranging from domiciliary care *in situ* to nursing home care
- the needs of family and informal carers.

The importance of training: sharing cross-agency experience and skills

Just as services are fragmented into specialisms, so too is training. There is a tendency to limit the scope of training to a specific client group, and little time is set aside to explore both the variances and commonalities associated with the lives of people with differing disabilities within that specific grouping. The term 'dual diagnosis' appears to be commonly accepted but is also given many divergent definitions, and the implications of 'dual diagnosis' are never truly explored. This seems especially true in relation to individual lifestyle and the process of ageing, although there is no evidence to suggest that this experience will be any different – or less individual – for people with disabilities than it will be for people in the general population.

There is a great need within current services for people with learning disabilities for training in anti-ageist practice, in order to prevent discriminatory working practice and to recognise, and positively acknowledge, the changes inherent in the ageing process. There is also a need for training in lifespan issues, such as moving from a family home, retirement, bereavement, loss of memory and changes in physical and mental health, which can only assist the effective support of older people with learning disabilities as they experience critical transitions. There is scope for training in reminiscence, personal biography and life review therapy.

> *'There is no method of therapeutic practice that cannot be applied to work with older people provided, as with clients of other ages, the method selected is appropriate to the abilities and wishes of the user, the experience of the worker and the nature of the identified problem.'* (Hughes ,1995 p106)

It should not be necessary to look far for this training; there is a wealth of it among the current specialisms, and this existing knowledge can simply be adapted and applied to the specific issue of older people with learning disabilities. The key lies in inter-agency collaboration, joint working and the sharing of existing experience, skills and knowledge.

Summary

Suggested principles of good practice in the design and provision of services for older people with learning disabilities

- Identify, as well as predict, actual, as well as perceived, future need specifically with reference to accessible housing, social and healthcare needs.
- Consider the appropriateness of existing service provision, both for people with learning disabilities and for older people, and identify service deficit in both areas with relation to older people with learning disabilities.
- Consider ageing *in situ,* environmental adaptation and the development of specialist domiciliary care agencies.
- Map and develop community links and routes of access to health, housing and social services.
- Develop staff training, specifically in the areas of anti-ageist practice and positive awareness of the ageing process.
- Recognise the quality of family care and consult the carers.

- Recognise the heterogeneity and unique personhood of the older person with learning disabilities, and tailor service provision through the individual planning process.
- Involve older service users with learning disabilities in service planning, in ways appropriate to their understanding, interest and motivation.
- Positively encourage inter-agency collaboration, joint working and the sharing of existing experience, skills and knowledge.

References

Baxter C, Poonia K, Ward L and Nadirshaw Z (1990) *Double Discrimination. Issues and services for people with learning disabilities from black and ethnic minority communities.* London. King's Fund.

Hughes B (1995) *Older People and Community Care – Critical theory and practice.* Buckingham: Open University Press.

O'Brien J and Tyne A (1981) *The Principles of Normalisation: A foundation for effective services.* London: Campaign for Mentally Handicapped People.

Robertson J, Moss S and Turner S (1996) Policy, services and staff training for older people with intellectual disability in the UK. *Journal of Applied Research in Intellectual Disability* **9** (2) 91–100.

Wolfensberger W (1985) *Reflections on the Status of Citizen Advocacy.* Toronto: National Institute of Mental Retardation.

Other learning disability resources available from Pavilion

Advances in Mental Health and Learning Disabilities

This quarterly Journal is a vital and pioneering source of information and research, and is the only UK Journal specific to the mental health needs of people with learning disabilities.

It integrates current research with practice and keeps professionals up to date with a variety of different perspectives, providing a forum for the debate of current issues and opinions.

Subscriptions start from just £55*.
View a sample article and subscribe online at **www.pavpub.com/amhldflyer**

Learning Disability Review

This quarterly Journal offers vital information and intelligence for people working in learning disability services. It bridges the experience of managers, practitioners, academics, users and carers to establish a constructive dialogue between different perspectives.

Learning Disability Review's primary focus is on learning disability services in the UK, but it also draws on international experience and practice, and recognises the scope of international learning and development.

Subscriptions start from just £55*.
View a sample article and subscribe online at **www.pavpub.com/ldrflyer**

For further information on Pavilion's portfolio of journals visit **www.pavpub.com/journals** or call **0870 890 1080**.

* Prices based on individual subscription rate. Individual subscriptions must be sent to a home address and paid from a personal account.

Learning Disability Today

Learning Disability Today magazine promotes better quality lifestyles for people with learning disabilities. Its unique focus on good practice in employment, health, leisure, education and housing helps readers to work towards genuinely inclusive connections and relationships within the community.

Each issue is full of inspiring features presented in a fun and lively format with a common-sense approach that readers can use to develop and maintain good practice in their own work. The magazine contains:

- a news update
- policy, practice and research discussions
- a focus on inclusion section
- reports on community relationships
- interviews
- regular perspectives from Scotland, Wales and the Valuing People Support Team
- news about events and resources.

Subscriptions start from just £45*.
View a sample article and subscribe online at **www.pavpub.com/ldtflyer**

* Price based on individual subscription rate. Individual subscriptions must be sent to a home address and paid from a personal account.

Pavilion training materials

Pavilion publishes over 150 training materials. Specialist areas include:
- learning disabilities
- mental health
- vulnerable adults
- substance misuse
- staff development
- children and young people.

Browse our portfolio and stay up to date with launches of the latest titles online at **www.pavpub.com/trainingmaterials**